PRAISE FOR *THE*

"In this impassioned and unfor[...] i M.
Savage explores the joy, beauty, and sadness that fill the lives of three
generations of women, some who love too much, and others struggling to love and be loved. Telling her own astonishing story, along
with her mother's and grandmother's, Savage's essays are filled with
the hard-earned wit and wisdom of a writer on a revelatory journey
that makes us laugh out loud while also moving us to tears. You
will read these essays again and again just to remain a bit longer in
Savage's delightful and healing company."

—Edwidge Danticat, author of *Brother, I'm Dying*
and *Everything Inside*, winner of the
PEN/Malamud Award for Excellence in the Short Story,
the National Book Critics Circle Award, the Story Prize,
and the Vilcek Prize in Literature

"Throughout, Savage writes as if speaking with a friend, relating her
experiences and that of others with sincerity. Readers of all back-
grounds are certain to appreciate her struggles and ability to cope
with the challenges she has faced. Raw, honest, and heartbreaking."

—*Kirkus Reviews*

"As someone who was raised by both my mother and my grandmother, I was laid bare by Jodi Savage's tender and tumultuous
recounting of her relationships with her mother and grandmother.
The moving essays in *The Death of a Jaybird* are at once beautifully
singular and representative of Black women's experiences coping
with love, loss, and grief."

—Deesha Philyaw, author, *The Secret Lives of Church Ladies*,
winner of the PEN/Faulkner Award for Fiction,
the Story Prize, LA Times Book Prize, and finalist for the
National Book Award for Fiction

"It's one thing to grieve one's mother after she has died; it's quite another to grieve her even as she lives. In this witty and moving collection centered on the complicated love among three generations of Black women, Jodi Savage does both with compassion and grace. *The Death of a Jaybird* is a timely reminder about the power of narrative to soothe our souls."

—Kim McLarin, author of
Everyday Something Has Tried to Kill Me and Has Failed

"*The Death of a Jaybird* is an exquisite and moving meditation on mothering and care across generations, on the complicated power of Black spiritualities and communities, and on resiliency in the face of trauma, illness, and grieving. Savage offers an unforgettable portrait of Black Pentecostal faith through her account of her grandmother's life, love, and lessons."

—Judith Weisenfeld, Agate Brown and
George L. Collord Professor of Religion and chair,
Department of Religion, Princeton University

"Jodi Savage's debut essay collection is a moving testament to her matriarchal lineage and a refreshingly honest account of what it's like to move through grief, love, and resilience. She writes about the complicated spaces one occupies as a daughter and granddaughter with grace, wit, and a faith that can only be found in words."

—Michele Filgate, editor of
What My Mother and I Don't Talk About

The
Death
of a
Jaybird

HARPER ● PERENNIAL

NEW YORK • LONDON • TORONTO • SYDNEY • NEW DELHI • AUCKLAND

The Death of a Jaybird

Essays on Mothers and Daughters and the Things They Leave Behind

Jodi M. Savage

HARPER PERENNIAL

"What If: On Black Lives and Mental Health" was previously published in *Catapult*; "Searching for Salvation at Antioch" was previously published in *Kweli Journal*; "How to Attend a Black Funeral" was previously published in the *VIDA Review*; portions of "I'm Too Pretty to Die Tonight" and "Running Out of Time" were previously published in *MadameNoire* as "Frankie and Cheryl: On Loving and Losing Mothers To Drug Addictions."

HarperCollins books may be purchased for educational, business, or sales promotional use. For information, please email the Special Markets Department at SPsales@harpercollins.com.

FIRST EDITION

Designed by Jen Overstreet
Title page illustration © Morphart Creation/Shutterstock

Library of Congress Cataloging-in-Publication Data

Names: Savage, Jodi M., 1978- author.
Title: The death of a jaybird : essays on mothers and daughters and the
    things they leave behind / Jodi M. Savage.
Other titles: Essays on mothers and daughters and the things they leave
    behind
Description: First edition. | New York, NY : HarperPerennial, [2023] |
    Summary: "Reminiscent of The Year of Magical Thinking and Somebody's
    Daughter, a deeply empathetic and often humorous collection of essays
    that explore the author's ever-changing relationships with her
    grandmother and mother, through sickness and health, as they experience
    the joys and challenges of Black American womanhood"— Provided by
    publisher.
Identifiers: LCCN 2023017893 (print) | LCCN 2023017894 (ebook) | ISBN
    9780063276086 (print) | ISBN 9780063276093 (ebook)
Subjects: LCSH: Savage, Jodi M., 1978- | Savage, Jodi M., 1978— Family. |
    African American women—New York (State)—New York—Biography. | African
    American women—Social conditions. | African American women—Health and
    hygiene. | Breast—Cancer—Patients—Biography. | African Americans—New
    York (State)—New York—Biography. | Brooklyn (New York,
    N.Y.)—Biography. | New York (N.Y.)—Biography. | Grief.
Classification: LCC F128.57.S38 A3 2023 (print) | LCC F128.57.S38 (ebook)
    | DDC 305.48/896073—dc23/eng/20230725
LC record available at https://lccn.loc.gov/2023017893

23 24 25 26 27 LBC 5 4 3 2 1

For

My grandmother, Annie Lee "Granny Poo" McKinney
My mother, Cheryl Ann Savage
My godmother, Christine Jones

It is sheer good fortune to miss somebody long before they leave you.

—TONI MORRISON, *SULA*

Contents

1

What If:
On Black Lives and Mental Health

When I think of Black Lives Matter, I think of my grandmother. Shortly after her seventieth birthday, she begins calling 911 in the middle of the night to report invisible squatters and the children they leave in her care at our home. Although she is a Black woman who was born in segregated Florida, she has had a reverence for the police for as long as I can remember. "The cops used to ride behind me to make sure I got home safely," she often tells me about her nightly walks home from work when she was just twelve years old. If there were a picture of the holy trinity, Granny's would be a color portrait of Jesus, President Barack Obama, and a police officer.

Granny donates small amounts of money to different police benevolent associations. In turn, they mail her gifts of appreciation like pink mailing labels pre-printed with her name and address in fancy calligraphy fonts, or calendars where each month displays a different profile and picture of an officer killed in the line of duty. Sometimes I wonder whether these organizations are even legit, but the lifetime supply of pretty labels makes it worth the risk.

When I think of Black Lives Matter, my mind wanders back to the night I awake to find a white police officer standing over my bed saying, "Ma'am, your grandmother called us. Do you mind if we take a look around?" *Do I really have a choice?* I think as I look up at the blond-haired, crew cut–wearing, broad-chested man standing in my bedroom. Granny has called 911 and already let him into our home and my bedroom. I'm not sure what mortifies me more: the fact that a cop is standing in my bedroom in the middle of the night while Granny yells *Are you okay?* at me from downstairs; or that a stranger is seeing me in my bedtime glory—a white headscarf with black polka dots; a green clay mask on my face; red plaid pajama pants; and a hole-riddled, used-to-be-orange-ten-years-ago T-shirt with the Serenity Prayer written on the front. Serenity is just what I need.

"My grandmother sees people who aren't really here," I tell the officer. He still searches my bedroom, and the two adjoining rooms that house a walk-in closet and a makeshift library Granny created for me several years ago. The invisible people have absconded with their children before the officer's arrival. The officer and I go back downstairs to talk to Granny. She is still waiting by the front door, her brown skin sweaty and her dark brown, straight, shoulder-length wig disheveled from the night's excitement. "I'll drive around the block a few times to see if they're still in the area," the officer tells Granny to ease her fears.

Unlike Granny, I have always felt uneasy about police. I don't espouse her *the cops are your friends* outlook. In 1999, I marched through New York City streets with hundreds of other Columbia University students to protest New York City police officers' shooting of West African immigrant Amadou Diallo. I wore a white label with "41" written in black magic marker taped to my bookbag strap for a whole year. I wanted every person I encountered to remember the forty-one times cops shot Mr. Diallo on his front stoop. I am still horrified when I think of Abner Louima, the Haitian man whom police tortured and sodomized with a toilet plunger in the bathroom of a Brooklyn precinct in 1997. I remember Rodney King, a black man whom Los Angeles police officers beat beyond recognition in 1991. I watched in shock when the officers were acquitted and riots erupted in LA.

And then there are the casual indignities boys in my family endure at the hands of police. Like the numerous times police stop my teenage cousins and ask them for IDs and their reasons for being in a certain neighborhood. A certain white neighborhood. A certain white neighborhood in which they reside. Even in a post-slavery, post-racial America, and long before Trayvon Martin crossed a fatal path with George Zimmerman, Black folks have needed manumission papers to be in their own neighborhoods. No, the police are not part of my holy trinity.

Eleanor Bumpurs
Sixty-six-year-old Black woman
Diagnosis: Psychosis
Bronx, New York
October 29, 1984

Eleanor has not paid rent in four months and owes $394.60. The New York City Housing Authority calls the police to evict Eleanor from her apartment. She doesn't open the door. The cops bust in. Eleanor charges towards the cops with a knife, they say. There is a struggle. An officer blasts two shots into Eleanor's right hand and chest. The shooter is acquitted. Two Social Services supervisors are demoted for failing to request proper psychiatric assistance and an emergency rent grant for Eleanor. The police shoot Eleanor like a rabid dog in the street—over $394.60.

Granny always shows signs that she is unraveling. Sometimes she chases the invisible people around the house, yelling at them to get out. I am afraid she will trip while chasing them up and down the stairs. Other nights, she is calmer but equally delusional, like the night I arrive home and she tells me, "He was cold, so I put a jacket on him."

"Who is cold?" I ask her.

"The little boy," she says. She is pointing to the banister, over which she has draped her pink and gray jacket. I don't tell Granny that the banister is not a little boy, because challenging her will only upset her. And it's been a long day at work.

She sometimes feeds the intruders, like the night I walk into the dining room and see four plates set out on the table. Each one contains potato chips and Oreo cookies. And she has set a glass of juice beside each plate. "The children were hungry," Granny explains.

"If they're still hungry later, you can feed them then," I reply and empty the dishes.

On one of these nights full of signs, Granny calls 911 again. Two cops arrive—one Black and one white. This is the first time a non-white officer has ever come. I don't remember the Black officer's name, but he looks young—much younger than the white officer. He has an angular, chiseled jaw and square chin. He remains quiet. I don't remember the white officer's face, his features merging into the countless others who have visited our home. But his name has a -shek at the end. I remember thinking that his name reminds me of "Damashek," the name of one of my elementary school teachers, so I name him Officer Damashek.

"Let's talk over here," I say to Officer Damashek while Granny continues talking excitedly about the squatters to the young Black officer. Granny is very defensive. I can't let her hear me tell the officer she's seeing things again. We stop in front of my neighbor's house next door. "My grandmother has been experiencing hallucinations for the last few months," I tell him. "They began after she fell at church."

"Does she have dementia?" Officer Damashek asks.

"I don't know. She refuses to go to the doctor."

"Jodi, don't lie! We can't get help if you lie!" Granny yells as she stands in front of our house. *Must you be so loud at one o'clock in the morning? Must the entire neighborhood hear our melodrama?* I try to telepathically ask Granny.

"Do you think she'll go to the hospital tonight?" Officer Damashek asks.

"I have no idea. But, you can try," I answer, my voice a mixture of sleep deprivation and resignation.

Officer Damashek walks back over to Granny and the Black officer.

"Ma'am, if we take the children to the hospital, will you go with them to make sure they're okay?" he asks Granny.

"Oh yes. Thank you, Jesus," she replies. Granny's prayers have been answered. She is relieved that her phantom children will be helped. I too am relieved, and hopeful that a doctor will finally be able to name the culprit responsible for Granny's forgetfulness and nighttime intruders. I grab some things from the house so that Granny and I won't show up to the hospital looking like a pair of homeless people: shoes, her medications, her butter pecan–flavored Ensure drink and Oreo cookies (like a child, Granny must always have snacks), and the house keys. I rush back outside before Granny changes her mind.

Granny and I sit in the ambulance as the police officers and paramedics exchange information.

"Where are the children?" Granny asks me.

"They're in the police car in front of us," I reply. Officer Damashek is a good teacher and I am a quick study. That answer satisfies her for the moment. We arrive at Jamaica Hospital. Although we used to always pass it as we rode the Q24 bus on our way to church in Queens, this is my first time here.

"Where are the children?" Granny asks again as the paramedics wheel her into the emergency room on the stretcher.

"They're in the pediatric emergency room next door," I say while pointing to a door adjoining the lobby.

"I think y'all just told me that to get me to go to the hospital," she says. I laugh. How quickly and suddenly the pendulum swings from delusion to lucidity.

"Well, you needed to come here anyway so you can rest," I answer. Never admit a lie. Just distract. And she does need to rest. Her late nights of screaming at the invisible people and calling the police have taken their toll, robbing her of sleep and leaving dark circles under her eyes. She sleeps through our entire ER visit. Several hours, X-rays, and conversations later, the doctor has an answer: vascular dementia. Numerous ministrokes over time have damaged her brain and are causing the hallucinations. As the sun rises the next morning, I call my boss from the ER to explain that I will not be coming to work that day. With a prescription for Seroquel and a referral to her primary care physician in hand, Granny and I take a cab home. I am relieved that Granny can come back home and is not placed in a psychiatric hospital or nursing home.

I keep meaning to search through my old journals, hoping I wrote down Officer Damashek's real name because I want to thank him. I want to thank him for seeing Granny not as a threat, but for who she really is: sick, afraid, frustrated, human.

Granny's 911 calls always scare me. I'm afraid the cops will fine us as punishment for Granny's making false police reports. Afraid the cops will take Granny away from me, separate us. I'm afraid they'll tell me, "It's clear you can't take care of her or adequately supervise her." Granny raised me. She brought me home from the hospital when I was a newborn. When it became clear that my mother's crack cocaine addiction wasn't a temporary phase, Granny filed an application with the Kings County Surrogate's Court to become my legal guardian. It has always been just the two of us.

I am also relieved that our police encounters have been pretty unremarkable—as unremarkable as one can be when chasing invisible people.

When I think of Black Lives Matter, I think of the Christmas Eve Granny calls 911 to report that she smells smoke and sees dead bodies lying on the floor. I am at work, unable to protect her. Unable to hold her hand while explaining, "Excuse me, officer. My grandmother sees people who aren't really here." Cop cars, ambulances, and fire trucks arrive at our house. Granny is frightened and begins to cry. She has forgotten where she placed her keys. The firemen break the lock on our front gate. When they enter, there is no smoke. No dead bodies. Just Granny. The authorities separate Granny and me—on Christmas Eve.

The police say Granny has to go to the hospital. The ambulance takes her to the psychiatric ER at Brookdale Hospital, and my neighbor Gail rides with Granny so that she will not be alone. But visitors aren't allowed in the psych ER. I visit Granny when she is transferred to the geriatric psych unit at Beth Israel hospital three days later. I cry when I see her, so helpless and confused. She is still talking about the invisible people at home. Her matching dark chocolate–colored velour shirt and pants have stains on them. Her nose and the surrounding skin are peeling and her lips are chapped. *How are these doctors helping her?* I wonder. After two weeks and numerous tests, the doctors find the real culprit: Alzheimer's disease with psychotic features.

When I think of Black Lives Matter, I revisit that day in the Dominican hair salon around the corner from our house. *I need to hurry up and get home,* a nagging inner voice warns as the stylist removes rollers from my hair. I rush out of the salon, my freshly curled hair not yet blown straight.

"Help! The voodoo man is trying to kill me," I hear Granny yell as I walk down the street. I walk faster and then I sprint the rest of the way home. A small tribe surrounds Granny on our front porch. Her home attendant attempts to console her in Spanglish with soft words and pats. Our neighbors try to reason with her through her tears.

"Do you really think we'd let people stay in your house and hurt you?" someone asks her. Granny stops to think.

"No, I guess not," she replies. But she won't move, still too afraid to go back inside. And then I call 911, because I don't know what else to do. Because Granny's anti-psychotic meds aren't working. Because the cops always know how to make her feel safe. This is the first time I have made this call. An ambulance arrives and takes her to the psych ER at Brookdale Hospital. Three days later, she is then transferred to the geriatric psych unit at Kingsbrook Jewish Medical Center. The doctors change her medications. Granny returns home two weeks later.

Michael Noel
Thirty-two-year-old Black man
Diagnosis: Paranoid Schizophrenia
St. Martinville, Louisiana
December 21, 2015

Michael's mother sees the signs, the signs that he is about to lose it again. He is agitated. Kicks an ironing board. Knocks over an ashtray. She waits until Michael leaves the house and then calls 911. She has made this call many times before. Just last week, Michael told police that he speaks to Jesus Christ. The coroner's office issues a protective order so the police can take Michael to the mental hospital. "Murderers!" Michael yells as the two white officers attempt to enter his house that evening. They wrestle Michael to the floor. They struggle and get one handcuff on him. Then, they take him down like a criminal on the run. One shot to the chest. In the living room. In front of his mother and aunt.

The coroner's office issued a protective order.

But it didn't protect him from death.

Maybe Michael really did talk to Jesus.

Maybe Jesus tried to warn him.

Maybe Jesus met him.

At the coroner's office.

When I think of Black Lives Matter, I think of my grandmother and I wonder. What if Granny were taller? Heavier? What if she were younger? A man? What if the cops had found her ranting and raving while wielding the long, skinny iron pole we keep by the front door? The same pole she used to swing at grown men who tried to flirt with me as a young girl.

LAVALL HALL
TWENTY-FIVE-YEAR-OLD BLACK MAN
DIAGNOSIS: SCHIZOPHRENIA
MIAMI GARDENS, FLORIDA
FEBRUARY 15, 2015

Lavall's mother awakens to find him outside, almost naked and holding a metal broom handle. She calls the police at five a.m. because she doesn't know what else to do. Because the cops always know how to make things better. Just a week ago, they had taken him to the mental hospital.

"I'm scared. Please don't hurt my baby," she says.

"Get on the fucking ground or you're dead," one officer yells at Lavall.

Five fatal shots pierce his body.

I wonder. What if Granny had grabbed a weapon to protect herself from the invisible people? A weapon like the yellow baseball bat she sometimes swings at the people in her TV. "Get outta here," she yells at her reflection in the black television screen. I take the bat from her and hide it in my bedroom to save the invisible people and our furniture.

DEBORAH DANNER
SIXTY-SIX-YEAR-OLD BLACK WOMAN
DIAGNOSIS: SCHIZOPHRENIA
BRONX, NEW YORK
OCTOBER 18, 2016

Neighbors call 911 because Deborah is acting erratically. Officers arrive. This is not the first time they have been called to her home. She is agitated. To Deborah, these officers are unwelcome guests. Invisible intruders made visible. She grabs a pair of scissors and then a baseball bat. She swings at an officer, they say. He shoots her two times.

Deborah and Eleanor are killed in the same month, thirty-two years apart. Two shots each. Same age. Same borough. A painful history repeated.

ANNIE LEE MCKINNEY
(AKA GRANNY)
SEVENTY-FOUR-YEAR-OLD BLACK WOMAN
DIAGNOSIS: ALZHEIMER'S DISEASE WITH PSYCHOTIC SYMPTOMS
BROOKLYN, NEW YORK
JUNE 27, 2011

I make one last 911 call. I am at work and Granny is with her home attendant. The home attendant says Granny is out of it and not herself. Granny is unable to feed herself. She is lethargic and talking strangely. "Put my grandmother on the phone," I say in a panic. Granny's speech is slurred. I call 911. I then call my neighbor and ask her to go check on Granny and wait for the ambulance to arrive. I leave work and rush to Kingsbrook Hospital, where they are taking

Granny. "Get off of me! I'm not going to lay here and let you kill me," she yells at the nurses in the emergency room, refusing to let them touch her. Perhaps she thinks the invisible people have followed her to the hospital. I try to calm her down and convince her that no one is going to hurt her. Once she is admitted, Granny continues fighting the nurses. They wrap restraints around Granny and tie them to the bed to prevent her from getting up. One day after being hospitalized, doctors place her on a respirator because she is having difficulty breathing.

"She's a miracle," a doctor tells me when Granny is taken off the respirator one week later. The doctors still don't know what caused her respiratory distress or the symptoms that landed her in the hospital. *Perhaps her Alzheimer's just advanced suddenly*, they tell me. *It happens sometimes*. This doesn't comfort me. *Maybe her body couldn't metabolize all of her medications*, they add. But I want to believe in magic and happy endings. We are optimistic that Granny will come back home once she receives feeding therapy and relearns how to swallow.

"She was able to swallow when she was home," I tell her doctor. "What happened?"

"With Alzheimer's patients, either they use it or lose it," he replies. "If they stop using a particular skill, even for a short period of time, they may forget it," he adds. Alzheimer's is such a sneaky thief.

Granny is transferred to a regular hospital room.

"In three weeks, it'll all be clear," she tells me one day while lying in her bed. I'm not sure she has spoken or that I've heard her correctly. Other than screaming at nurses and talking to her dead sisters and mother, she has barely spoken since being hospitalized.

"What did you say?" I ask her.

"In three weeks, it'll all be clear."

"What do you mean by that?"

"I don't know," she replies in a soft childlike voice. She doesn't say anything else.

Granny is discharged from the hospital and admitted to a nursing home two weeks after being hospitalized. She never begins feeding therapy because she is either unwilling or unable to follow the therapists' directions.

And then she develops pneumonia in both lungs. Rapidly multiplying bacteria spread throughout her bloodstream and her body goes into septic shock.

Every time I touch Granny, her heart monitor beeps faster. When I touch her right leg, she raises it and turns towards me. She opens her mouth wide, unable to scream because she is intubated. But her arched eyebrows and the grimace on her face let me know she is in pain. Granny is right. It is starting to become clear. I think Jesus talks to Granny. Jesus is trying to warn us.

I look for Granny's doctor, but can't find her. So, I wait.

"Can I sign those papers the social worker spoke to me about?" I ask when she returns to Granny's room. "I don't want her to suffer," I whisper. I can't hold back my tears.

"I understand," the doctor replies. I sign the do-not-resuscitate order that night.

My friend Jennifer is with me. We sing and read Bible scriptures to Granny. And I talk to her, even if she can't answer. Even if I'm not sure she hears me.

"Thank you for being the best grandmother I could ask for," I tell her as she struggles to breathe. I stroke her chin and forehead, the only places on her body I can touch that don't hurt. "I love you. It's okay if you need to leave me now."

The next day, two weeks after Granny's spontaneous utterance, I am on my way to see her. My phone rings at 12:19 p.m. as I rush through the double doors to the Intensive Care Unit. It is Granny's doctor calling.

"Ms. Savage, I am sorry to inform you . . ."

"Don't say it. I know. I'm here," I say to the doctor. Our eyes lock as he sits at the workstation outside Granny's room with the phone still to his ear. Granny is still warm. I am surprised at how peaceful she looks, her skin color having changed from a fever-induced red hue to its natural golden brown state. Her amber-colored eyes have dulled to a gray, her fire extinguished. "Sweetie, it's finally over," I say as I hold her swollen hand and stroke her small face. I close her eyes.

Death is never welcomed, nor easy. But how one dies matters. I am grateful. Grateful I had a chance to say goodbye. Grateful Granny did not die like a criminal on the run or a rabid dog in the street. Death could have come by bullet, on our front porch or in our home. Who would bear witness? Just two Black women in the middle of the night—one young, one old. No smartphone cameras or Facebook Live to capture the last moments. In another time, Granny could have been another name. Another hashtag created. Another life stolen. I am grateful that death chose, instead, to visit Granny in a quiet hospital room. On a warm sunny afternoon. The last Monday in June.

2

Searching for Salvation at Antioch

Granny raised me on mustard greens, hot water cornbread, and a super-sized portion of Jesus. Although I mastered the Rubik's Cube of rules for sanctified living, religion robbed me of my voice and left shame in its place. You could say that it all started with my teenage neighbor Bobby.

When I was a kid, I let Bobby paint my fingernails red. I knew it was a sin by Pentecostal standards, but my nails looked so pretty and shiny in the sunlight. A few days later, our neighborhood had our annual block party. Everyone had moved their cars off our Brooklyn street that morning; one end was blocked off with an Oldsmobile Cutlass Supreme and the other with a Nissan Maxima. We played in the street all day until late into the night—volleyball, tag, double Dutch, hide-and-seek. Folks played spades and dominoes on the sidewalks; roamed from yard to yard sampling each other's food; and blasted reggae, reggaeton, old school R&B, and hip hop from various speakers all at the same time.

As I played across the street from my house, Bobby barreled into me on his bike. His front wheel and handlebars collided with my groin and stomach, sending me flying several feet away. I limped home to tell Granny what happened. She suddenly noticed my red fingernails for the first time. Again, we were Pentecostal, which meant we weren't allowed to wear fingernail polish. Anything red was considered to be a special kind of sinful—carnality of the whorish variety. Instead of consoling me, Granny whipped me with an extension cord. That was the day I learned that one's own pain is secondary to religious dogma.

I learned to keep quiet when people hurt me, or else risk punishment for revealing something far worse—something sinful. Something nasty and ungodly that might send me straight to the pits of hell and make Granny stop loving me. And so I never told Granny about our teenage neighbor Michael, who always climbed on top of me in my bed whenever he babysat me.

For Granny, faith was her salvation. It had given her a new life when she moved from Florida to New York in the 1950s to work as a live-in domestic for a white family in Jericho, Long Island. With no family or friends in her new city, fellow church members became her surrogate family. When my mother was born, Granny was twenty-three and unmarried—circumstances that were still taboo in 1960. *We didn't even know she was pregnant until after your mother was born,* an aunt told me. *I didn't even know I was pregnant,* Granny used to say. *The doctors said I had a tumor or some kind of growth.* But perhaps she was too ashamed to admit her pregnancy, distance from her family and her petite frame allowing her to hide it. Her church family served as friends, babysitters, and godparents. And that support system lasted for decades. One of my godmothers, who is still alive, christened me more than twenty years after she originally christened my mother.

Granny eventually became a licensed evangelist. This was a far cry from the version of herself she'd left in Riviera Beach, Florida—where she chain-smoked, got into fights, and frequented a bar called Snook's every day.

Although Granny frequently preached in churches in New York and elsewhere, she wasn't choosy about where she found her flock. She preached everywhere—trains, street corners, wherever there were souls that needed to be saved. She used to preach on our front porch while I passed out sandwiches and fruit punch to people who stopped to listen to her. She'd stand there, the overhead light shining down on her in the darkness as if she were an angel, and belt out fervent exhortations of grace and redemption. Her pop-up congregation sat on their bicycles or leaned against our wrought-iron fence munching and listening. Granny's insistence on feeding people during her porch sermons reminded me of the Biblical story in which Jesus and his disciples fed thousands of people with only five loaves of bread and two fish. I suppose a dose of Jesus is best served on a full stomach. Pentecostal preachers are loud and theatrical, and Granny was no exception. During these porch sermons, she would pray, sing, and clap her thin, small hands loudly. She frequently interjected her prayers and singing with excited utterances of "heeee caaa shon da laaa bo seeekiaaah!" or other variations thereof while she spoke in tongues.

No neighborhood gathering was ever complete without a prayer from Granny, and most folks indulged her. Sometimes she carried her bottle of blessed oil from house to house, anointing neighbors' doors and gates. Other times, a simple prayer would do. During a block party one summer, Granny decided to pray for all the kids. However, my neighbor Steve was not on board with that plan. Steve, who was in high school like me, was short and round. Despite his heft, he ran away from Granny at the speed of an Olympic athlete. In response, Granny did what any self-respecting Bible thumper would do. She chased him down the middle of the street with her Bible, while dodging playing kids and a volleyball net. She finally caught Steve at the end of the street. You can't outrun Jesus. Or Granny.

The summer after my first year of law school, Granny went with me to the doctor. Although we were in the middle of a heat wave, my chest was congested, my voice hoarse, and my ears stopped up. When my name was finally called, she waited with me in the examining room.

The nurse practitioner—a tall, surly looking white woman with blond hair—came in with a medical student. The student, a Black woman, looked as if she were fresh out of undergrad. I explained my symptoms to the NP. She then asked me some background questions. *Are you allergic to any medications?* (No.) *Are you currently on any medications?* (No.) *When was your last period?* (I never remembered so I made up the date.) *Is there a possibility you may be pregnant?* (Not unless I was the Virgin Mary 2.0.) *Have you ever been sexually molested or raped?* (Silence.) No one had ever asked me this. And then the tears came, heavy and uncontrollable. Granny stood still, her eyes wide. "Maybe you should wait outside," the NP told her.

Take a deep breath. The intern had a *Damn, medical school didn't cover this* look on her face before she, too, left the office. She returned with some Kleenex and a hug. "I'm so sorry," she said. *What happened?* I was there for my self-diagnosed ear infection and cold. What did their questions have to do with anything? And then I told them about Michael. *How old were you?* (Really young. Eight or nine or seven.) *Did he penetrate you?* (I don't think so. Not completely. I wasn't sure.) I had blocked the abuse out for years, my memory only being triggered when I began dating a guy my junior year of college. Besides, I had other experiences of sexual abuse to fill the void. *You should get a GYN exam.* Granny had taken me for an exam when I started my period at nine years old. I was so terrified of anything entering me that I hadn't been to the gynecologist since that first visit. I didn't have an ear infection or cold after all. I had bronchitis and a bad case of repressed memories.

Granny and I walked home in silence. As soon as we arrived, I went straight to bed and cried some more. She brought me juice and crackers, and sat beside me on the bed.

"Who was it?" she asked. I couldn't bear to tell her that a neighbor's son had molested me. I didn't want her to live with the guilt of knowing this had happened in our own home. She might never forgive herself. I thought the abuse would sound less intrusive, less harmful, if I only told her about Natasha, another neighbor who sexually abused me whenever I stayed at her house overnight while her parents or older sister babysat me. Granny never let me spend the night when Natasha's mom worked the graveyard shift. "You don't need to be alone with no man," she would say. As strict as Granny was, she still couldn't protect me.

"I figured it might be her," Granny replied. How long had she "figured" this? And why? Was it because I had spent so much time at Natasha's house? Had I shown signs?

"I hope you don't blame me."

"I don't," I reassured her.

But I did blame her—not for failing to prevent the abuse, but for creating an environment in which I didn't feel safe enough to tell her the truth. And what use would blaming her do? How could I say I was so afraid of the sinfulness of sex that I was willing to hide my own abuse for years? What would I have gained by saying that her fanatical, puritanical religion had terrified me so much that I was afraid of being "bad" or "dirty"? Throughout my life I have struggled with believing I deserve to hold people accountable for hurting or disappointing me.

Granny had been molested by her stepfather when she was twelve years old. Although her mother didn't believe her, her grandmother and a teacher did. The adult me wants to think Granny would have believed me had I told her about the abuse. But I never forgot the red fingernail polish and the judgment that came after. Granny and I never spoke of my sexual abuse again. In life, we must learn to accept the apologies we will never get.

Growing up, religion was always about rules—following the ones that would gain God's (or some man's) favor, not breaking others so as not to incur God's wrath. I spent a lot of time learning these rules: Friday night service; Sunday school, Sunday morning service, *and* Sunday night service; communion and foot washing service once a month; midnight prayer service during the week; an occasional all-night tarry service; church conventions in other states during the summer; and choir rehearsals once a month. My life, social circle, and sense of right and wrong all revolved around church. The church considered it a sin for women to do anything that might invite sexual desire from men; or might enable us to revel in our own bodies and femininity. No makeup, lipstick, fingernail polish, or jewelry (except wedding rings) were allowed, lest we draw men under our Jezebel spell. Women couldn't wear pants because God apparently had a strong aversion to women wearing men's clothing—and because pants showed off the irresistible curves of our legs and hips. Our dresses and skirts had to fall to the knee or lower, and we couldn't have slits in our skirts so as to prevent men from looking straight up to the cracks of our behinds. The church preferred women to hide our bodies, rather than requiring that men regulate their own behavior and imaginations.

Whenever women entered our church, we had to cover our heads. Our usual coverings were round, lace doily-like cloths with attached combs to hold them in place. We had them in different colors to match our outfits. For special occasions we had head coverings that were white, flowy, shoulder-length scarves that covered our entire heads. These were made of lace, satin, or cotton. We only wore them during communion, on Pentecost Sunday, and during the fifty days of consecration between Easter and Pentecost Sunday. The cotton scarves were my least favorite because they made my head sweat and dried my hair out; the lace ones were prettier and offered lots of ventilation.

Women were even restricted in how we wore our hair beneath the head coverings. We couldn't wear braids, although I've since forgotten the origin of this religious tenet. Given the thickness of my hair, however, Granny was a lot more relaxed about the no-braids rule. She used to let our neighbors and family friends braid my hair in cornrows when I was a little girl. Sometimes they'd get extra fancy and add colored beads to the ends of my hair; small pieces of tin foil would hold them in place. In high school, Granny started letting me get my hair braided at African braiding salons.

The common denominator: women needed to be tamed in order to show we were even worthy of being in God's sight, let alone loved. I didn't understand how these "sins" made one unworthy of God's love and how their absence made one closer to God. Is God really that petty and bored?

The church did not police men's bodies and behavior. While women's actions were condemned, men's were ignored. Whenever an unmarried woman or teenage girl got pregnant, she became a pariah. The pastor would punish her by making her repent and sit in the back of the church for the duration of her pregnancy. She wasn't allowed to participate in any church activities. No singing in the choir, no serving on the usher board or the praise and worship team. It was as if her fornication were contagious, her presence a reminder of moral failure. But expectant, unwed fathers weren't shamed or even outed, as if the women had gotten pregnant by themselves. The fathers simply continued their lives—preaching, playing the drums or organ. They were boys continuing to be boys, their behavior and reputations unencumbered by rules of "godly" behavior.

The salacious sex scandals involving male pastors had all the makings of a chart-topping reality TV show before reality TV was a thing. For years, everyone knew our married pastor was sleeping with other women in the church. As a kid, I used to hear Granny and her friends gossiping about our pastor's mistresses and marital woes. One Sunday morning, while sitting in the alto section of the choir stand, I noticed a lot of commotion in the balcony. A group of men were wrestling with someone. I later learned that the detained man was married to our pastor's girlfriend. He had brought a rifle with a scope attached, and planned to send our pastor straight into the afterlife. A gun-toting husband was urgent enough for the church to convene a meeting. No kids were allowed, so my friends and I hung out at the nearby library until the meeting was over. The members voted to fire our pastor. He started another church close by and many people, including Granny and me, followed him. Had our pastor been a woman, he would not have received such loyalty and forgiveness.

I remember the day I became bitter towards religion and God. I was a freshman at Barnard College, and had regularly attended Pastor B's church for several months with one of Granny's friends. He was a popular Baptist pastor in Brooklyn who'd started off with one church and then founded a school and an organization made up of many member churches. His highly spirited preaching reminded me of the churches I'd grown up in. I also admired the fact that women at his church weren't just ushers, choir members, president of the hospitality board, or married to the ministers. His church had many women ministers who sat in the pulpit. Those women were some of the best preachers around. Many of the Baptist and Pentecostal churches I'd attended over the years didn't allow women ministers to sit in the pulpit or to perform such tasks as officiating at weddings and funerals. Pastor B's church seemed like a perfect combination of Jesus and feminism in action. On the Sunday I planned to become an official member of his church, Pastor B began his sermon by telling a story about a woman who had gone to her own pastor for counseling because her husband was beating her. Instead of encouraging the woman to leave her husband, the pastor instructed her to return home. Her husband later beat her to death. Although Pastor B admitted that the woman's pastor had been wrong for advising her to stay with her abuser, he also said it was okay for a man to beat his wife. He then began talking about other rights men had in marriage.

"You women say you don't wanna have oral sex. But you kiss and the mouth is dirty and doesn't even clean itself," Pastor B shouted from the pulpit as children and adults listened. "At least the vagina cleans itself." He was more explicit than any sex education class I had ever taken. "A woman cannot deny her husband sex," he continued.

"Amen! Preach, pastor!" the men in front of me yelled as they waved their hands and high-fived each other. *You muthafuckas cannot be serious,* I thought as I looked around at them with disgust. The faces of the older church mothers registered a collective *Now hold on just a damn minute* as they mumbled amongst themselves. And yet no one challenged Pastor B.

I slowly raised my hand. In case you're wondering, a Sunday morning sermon in a Black Baptist or Pentecostal church is not a Q & A session. It is not a Bible study class. You're supposed to just sit and listen, and let out an occasional *Glory!* Or *Hallelujah!* Or *You betta preach!* And when the organist starts playing the fast shoutin' music, you grab a tambourine or you get up and dance your best holy dance. But you do not raise your hand.

"Yes, young lady?" Pastor B asked me.

"If a husband forces his wife to have sex, wouldn't that be considered rape?" Surely, logic would prevail.

"How can you rape something that belongs to you?" he asked me in a very matter-of-fact manner. It wasn't really a question. *Something.* A thing, not an equal or human being. *That belongs to you.* A possession. I was stunned. Angry. I felt exposed and invisible. It was the first time I ever felt unsafe in a church. What kind of God sanctioned the abuse and rape of women? What kind of monster preached such things? And what kind of congregation thought such teachings were acceptable?

Pastor B's sermon seemed out of character. I had visited his church many times since I was a small child. One of my earliest church memories was of being at a tent revival, my legs swinging from a wooden chair as Pastor B sang in his robust tenor voice. His was a progressive church, far more liberal than the Pentecostal fundamentalist church I had grown up in. He had a large following and multiple churches. Some of my favorite women preachers held leadership positions in his church. Granny and her friends said Pastor B had caught his wife sleeping with another man shortly before that sermon—that his words were really the ramblings of a heartbroken husband. But such an explanation did not excuse his rant. If the rumors about his wife were true, his reaction was not surprising. Much of religion is a tower constructed to protect male egos and privilege.

Dissatisfied with his views and our exchange, I decided to write Pastor B a letter. But Granny disagreed with my course of action. "Don't do it. He knows the Bible better than you," she told me after receiving counsel from her pastor—her male pastor. "He'll chew you up and spit you out."

Her trembling voice let me know she wanted to protect me from being humiliated. But I was the girl who had fallen in love with feminism in junior high, when I read bell hooks's *Ain't I a Woman* for the first time. The kind of girl who had known since eleventh grade that I wanted to attend an all-women's college. I didn't need the Bible to tell me about my place in the world. And I was tired of keeping quiet about the things that hurt me.

Granny's reaction shocked me because I had always thought of her as a tough and fearless woman. She was my hero. She used to tell me how she had beat up a family member's husband because he was abusing her. Granny's twin brother reminisced about how she used to fight boys who bullied him in school. Years later, when Granny got saved, she became a rabble-rousing letter writer. Whenever she needed to tell a pastor something important, she would write him a letter or record her message on a cassette tape and hand deliver it to him. I was exactly who she had raised me to be. I don't know why she thought some justification for Pastor B's words would be found in the

Bible. Or why she didn't go with me to deliver my letter. Sometimes we must be our own hero.

In my best cursive penmanship, I wrote a nineteen-page letter to Pastor B titled "Amazing Disgrace." Undeterred by Granny, I returned the next Sunday to deliver my message. I handed him the letter as I walked by to put money in the offering plate. How ironic: me financially supporting a religious institution that did not support my human rights.

Wearing a broad smile, he began silently reading my letter from the pulpit as people passed by. Remembering the adage, "Start with the positives before you criticize," I began the letter by telling Pastor B why I had admired him and wanted to join his church.

The muscles in Pastor B's face tensed up and his smile began to fade. I recounted the story he had told us about the woman whose husband killed her. *If you believe that woman's pastor was wrong for telling her to return to her abusive husband, then how can you advocate for the rape, abuse, and oppression of women? Does God's grace not extend to women?* I've since forgotten how he justified domestic violence and rape, but not murder, how he condoned violence against women, but faulted his fellow clergyman for having advised a woman to return to such violence. Maybe my anger erased the memory of his explanation. In his theologically inspired hierarchy of violence, perhaps there's a threshold of acceptable abuse. Maybe you ought to beat a woman just enough for her to comply, but there is some point at which you can punch or slap a woman too hard or one too many times. A point at which you've gone too far. I've often wondered whether Pastor B was the pastor in his story, struggling to rationalize his way to a clear conscience.

Pastor B's face now looked as if he smelled raw meat that had been left outside all day. *Being a member of your church as a woman is as insane as me being a member of the KKK as a Black person.* I am unimpressed by mere representation; doctrine matters more. Women make up the majority of most Black churches. We fill choirs and usher boards and missionary committees. We are pastors and ministers. And yet many churches preach sexism and misogyny and violence towards women. I've often wondered what compels a woman to stay in a church like Pastor B's. Perhaps they justify it as they would staying in an abusive or dysfunctional romantic relationship. *I've invested too many years to just walk away.* Or *Any church is better than no church.* Maybe they tell themselves, *Every church will have something you dislike, so you might as well just embrace the good parts and ignore the bad.* More Black women are killed in the United States than any other racial group. Black women are also more likely to be physically and psychologically abused by our intimate partners. We experience rape and other forms of sexual or physical violence at disproportionately high rates. Black women cannot afford the gospel of misogyny.

Black women rightfully demand that people outside our communities recognize our humanity—white people, white feminists, police officers, politicians. But how often do we surrender our humanity to racial solidarity and the church and Jesus? The church taught me what it looks like when Black people, especially Black women, do not hold our institutions and our people accountable. The church taught me to walk away from things that no longer serve me.

Pastor B suddenly threw my letter to the ground. Later in the service, still overcome with indignation, he attempted to do what is commonly done to women who think for themselves—he berated me.

"Some of you think you know everything just because you've gone to college and can string a few sentences together," he told the congregation. I smiled to myself. Nineteen pages was more than "a few sentences." That was the last time I ever went to that church or attempted to join any other.

I spent years trying to follow the right formula to get into heaven. I was the perfect church kid. I swore off premarital sex. I overdosed on school gospel choirs, Bible scriptures, church revivals, and a tambourine I named after the Biblical prophet Miriam. But I did secretly listen to "worldly" music—the kind of music that made one worldly and well-rounded. I was in love with Tevin Campbell and his sweet voice. In junior high, I sang his song "Tomorrow" during my audition for the drama club. I was a screeching falsetto mess. The drama coach also coached the debate club. We both discovered that I was better suited to debating about the 4th Amendment's protection against unreasonable searches and seizures. Keith Sweat, Brandy, SWV, and Surface were also among my favorite artists. I either bought bootleg cassettes off the street, or recorded their songs when they came on WBLS, Hot 97, and 98.7 Kiss FM on the radio or television shows like *Video Music Box* with Ralph McDaniels and *Video Soul* with Donnie Simpson. I'd turn the music down low so Granny wouldn't hear. I once fell asleep listening to Quincy Jones's *Back on the Block* album. When I awoke the next morning, I discovered that Granny had confiscated the cassette tape and my Walkman while I was sleeping. I didn't find the tape until years later, after Granny passed away.

When I began college, I was shocked by how few Black students there were in comparison to my Brooklyn high school. I was so eager to meet other students who looked like me that I once walked up to a random group of Black students at Ollie's, a restaurant near campus, and shouted, "Excuse me, are y'all first years?" They were first years, and all but one of them ignored me for the rest of our time in college. A small group of us church-hopped in search of a Black community and the familiarity of our pre-college lives. One of my friends was Catholic so we visited a Catholic church, where we gawked at journalist Bryant Gumbel after the service. We also visited the historic Canaan

Baptist Church in Harlem, which reminded me of the churches I had attended all my life. I was so offended by the bus loads of white tourists who sat in the church's balcony that I later wrote a paper about it. Although having a designated tourist section minimized disruptions during the service, their presence felt sacrilegious. It felt as if we were animals being observed in our natural habitat or expected to perform tricks to entertain the white folks at a circus. We also joined the Barnard-Columbia Gospel Choir because we knew it was likely to be full of Black folks—and we were right. More than twenty years later, I'm still friends with many of the students I met in gospel choir.

Although our churchgoing routine didn't last long, and Pastor B's infamous sermon had left me jaded, I wanted to understand religion's influence over people. I took various religion classes, studied black liberation theology, and considered double majoring in religion. For my "Black Women's Religious Experiences" class, I designed and conducted a study that examined the ways in which Black women's religious beliefs affected their political and feminist views. But I didn't learn anything that would erase the cynicism and sense of betrayal Granny's faith had left me with. As I would with a school bully, I respected religion's power and kept my distance.

Whenever I went home for the weekend, Granny would make me go to church with her. "While you're in my house, you have to abide by my rules," she would tell me. By the time I graduated from college, I had stopped regularly going to church. But church was my earliest form of community. Church was inseparable from the person I loved most.

After Granny developed Alzheimer's disease, she began hallucinating. Her phantoms ranged from people having sex in our backyard, to the mafia having a sit-down in her bedroom, to a young man's funeral occurring in our closet. "He had AIDS," she whispered to me after one of these funerals. I had stopped taking her to church or to places with large crowds, because her hallucinations and delusions followed her. I never knew when she was going to start yelling at the invisible people. We once went to see her friend's grandson perform at Julliard. We'd taken Access-A-Ride, the ride-sharing service for people with disabilities, to and from the performance. On our way back home, there was only one other passenger in the van—a tall, well-dressed, elderly Black woman in possession of all her mental faculties. Granny yelled at the woman the entire ride about being in cahoots with the invisible people who were trying to take over our house.

"You oughtta be ashamed of yourself for trying to overthrow me," Granny said. "But God said, 'No weapon that is formed against me shall prosper!'" Even in her illness, God was her personal hit man.

"Granny, she doesn't know us," I said.

"Shut up. I know what I'm talking about." I shut up and gave the woman a sympathetic look. Thankfully, she never responded to Granny. We listened to her tirade for over an hour.

Although Granny didn't go to church often, she never lost her Pentecostal mojo. During a two-week hospital stay to assess the cause of her hallucinations, I worried that she would be anxious about being in a new environment. But she quickly slipped back into her familiar self. Like every smart inmate, Granny found a crew and established her leadership role among the unit's patients. She met with a small group every day in the dining room, where she prayed, gave short sermons, and counseled her fellow patients. She saw a need for hope and encouragement, and she filled it. Supply and demand economics apply even in the old folks' psych ward.

During one of my visits, I caught Granny holding one of her church services.

"Your grandmother really blessed me. She's a wonderful woman," a patient told me. She and the others were sitting at one of the dining room's round, light gray tables while Granny stood facing them.

"Here's my name. Please pray for me when you get out," another woman said as she handed Granny a piece of paper.

"I sure will," Granny answered with a smile. Her tone was benevolent, as if she were doling out blessings and forgiveness. I pictured her saying, "Go in peace and sin no more, my child," while making the sign of the cross. And then I remembered all those cans of ginger ale hidden in her nightstand drawer. I wondered if her parishioners had given them to her as offerings or to express their gratitude. The scene reminded me of those movies where the prisoner who's being released promises his homies left behind that he'll keep in touch or do some favor for them once he returns to the outside world. The freed prisoner usually leaves and never looks back. Granny probably wouldn't even remember them after being discharged. But it was fascinating to watch. Despite lingering somewhere between fantasy and reality, she was still a charismatic, Holy Ghost–loving preacher.

Granny's connection with God made her popular with the other patients, but it complicated matters with her doctors.

"She has religious ideations," a young white resident wearing a yarmulke said to me while discussing Granny's Alzheimer's diagnosis. "She says she's a prophet and that God talks to her."

Although I had my own conflicted relationship with religion, I resented that the doctor hadn't taken the time to learn about Granny. Instead, he had dismissed her beliefs. I needed to make the doctor see her.

"No, no, no. She has always been very religious—even before the hallucinations and delusions," I told him. Realizing how inadequate that explanation was, what I really wanted to say was, *Granny believing she's a prophet and that God talks to her is her normal level of crazy. That's her baseline. I can deal with God. It's all the other people who need to go.* The home invaders having oral sex in the recliner chair in Granny's bedroom? Those were the real culprits. The voodoo man hiding in the closet and bathtub? Evict him for good. The mafia, who regularly met in Granny's bedroom and who told her we could stay in our home? Tell them they don't make the rules and send them packing. I needed the doctor to focus on the real problem.

It was true that Granny had always referred to herself as a "prophet"—an oracle or a person to whom God speaks about things that will happen in the future. In the Pentecostal faith, prophets aren't just dead people you read about in the Bible. They are chosen by God and highly respected. Pentecostals view prophets as being extremely devoted to God, not delusional fanatics.

Granny's doctors might have committed her for life had I told them that, for as long as I could remember, she had engaged in a practice called "writing in the spirit." When writing in the spirit, Granny would compose passages in an unintelligible dialect of symbols, shapes, curves, and strokes that looked like a young child's scribblings. Although no one else could understand them, Granny said God revealed messages to her through the writing. She often hung pages of her writing in various places throughout our house—above doorways, on doors and walls—because she believed they would bring God's blessings and protection.

Other churchgoers viewed Granny's writing as a gift from God.

"Prophetess McKinney, write in the spirit and tell me what thus sayeth the Lord," one person or another would say to Granny whenever they wanted God's guidance. She would take out some paper, usually a black and white composition notebook—but any random piece of paper, even a napkin, would do—and she would silently begin writing until she felt God had revealed his intended message to her. To me and our community of faith, Granny's religious beliefs and practices were not "religious ideations"; they were her legacy.

In defending Granny's faith, I was trying to preserve what Alzheimer's had not yet seized. Even when her memory and sense of reality began to fail her, her faith remained unchanged. I was determined to cling to as much of the old her as possible.

Four years ago, almost three years after Granny's death and less than a year after I sold the home she and I had shared since I was a baby, I dreamt about Granny. In the dream, Granny sat in the dining room as I sat facing her from the adjoining living room.

"How do you feel about us moving?" I asked her.

"I feel good about it." Her voice sounded optimistic about the future.

"The house seems a lot bigger with all the stuff out of it," I added.

"Yeah, it does."

"Now, the new neighborhood is a lot busier than this one," I warned.

"Really?"

"Yeah. A *lot* busier."

"Okay. Well the first thing I'm gonna do is check out the . . ."

"The churches?" I completed her sentence. What else would she be interested in? Church was her life.

"Yeah. I wanna go to Antioch Baptist Church."

And then the dream ended.

I had never been to an Antioch Baptist Church; nor had Granny ever mentioned one. There was an Antioch on 125th Street in Harlem, near my college. I used to pass it whenever a friend and I cut class to go to M&G's Diner for some salmon, grits with scrambled eggs, and white toast, or whenever an old boyfriend and I went to mass at St. Joseph's. When I googled "Antioch Baptist Church," I discovered that there was also one in the Brooklyn neighborhood Bedford-Stuyvesant. It was founded by Reverend Moses Prophet Paylor in 1918. The likes of Reverend Martin Luther King, Jr.; Rosa Parks; Langston Hughes; and Aretha Franklin had visited the Bed-Stuy church over the years.

Not long after my dream, on my way to a book club meeting in Park Slope, I passed an Antioch AME Church. It was warm outside, so they had the doors open. I stood in the doorway and watched. Everyone was dressed in white, perhaps for communion, the pastor's anniversary, or Women's Day. An usher invited me in, but I declined, not wanting to be late. Our book club was going to discuss *Wave*, a memoir of loss by Sonali Deraniyagala. It wasn't a Baptist church, but it was close enough. It was a sign.

I visited the Antioch Baptist Church in Bed-Stuy the following Sunday. Just as intrigued by my dream as I was, my two friends and three of their children accompanied me. We didn't dress up for the occasion. We looked like lost tourists stopping in for directions and a place to rest. The church had all the splendor of a cathedral—with its high ceilings, arches and columns, stained glass windows, and wooden balconies—and the intimacy of a storefront church. The parishioners ranged from elderly Black women who reminded me of Granny with their fancy suits and big hats, to hospital employees fresh off work and still in their scrubs, folks in jeans, and at least one woman in flannel pajama pants. The come-as-you-are doctrine was in full effect. The kids gave a tribute to Nelson Mandela, and I sang along to the choir's familiar selections. As we sat in the back of the church, I felt love. I could feel Granny's spirit. I imagined her laughing in triumph and saying, "I'm gon' get you saved if it's the last thing I do."

Antioch was the kind of church I might like if I went regularly: politically aware, liberal, good singing and fast shoutin' music, and sermons that were equal parts fiery, scholarly, and practical. And its members were friendly. Church folks can be some of the meanest folks, especially if you sit in the seat they occupy every Sunday.

"Go to someone not sitting next to you and shake their hand," the pastor told the congregation. A man and woman from several rows ahead of us came back to shake our hands. And then one of my friends told the couple about my dream.

"Well God meant for you to be here," the man replied. Visiting Antioch was like going home. It was a little piece of Granny on Earth.

In grief, we look for ways to hold on to our loved ones. I use words to hold on to Granny. I read books about others who have lost people and things. I sift through Granny's old Bibles, reading scripture she underlined and the notes she made on napkins and in the margins. I flip through the notebooks she used to write in the spirit, running my fingers along the pages to feel her pen's indentations. If I can no longer hold her hands, at least I can feel what her hands created. Granny was obsessed with preserving the details of her life. She used to record everything—telephone conversations, church services, random conversations in the house. I sometimes listen to these old cassette tapes because her voice comforts me. One of my favorites is a recording from when I was a little girl. Granny and I are gossiping as I help her pick an outfit for church. And I think about my visit to Antioch. I'm sure if I look close enough, visit frequently enough, I'll find cracks in the foundation. Imperfect people. Intolerable doctrines and politics. But I'm not looking for Jesus or the church or a preacher to save me. I'm just trying to hold Granny close. And make peace with the ways in which her faith has been my curse and her legacy. I'm still searching for my own faith, my own kind of salvation.

3

How to Attend a Black Funeral

1. A Black funeral is not called a funeral. Rather, it is a home-going or homegoing service. A homegoing is a celebration of a person's life, a mourning for what has been lost, and a going away party all wrapped in one. At a homegoing, folks celebrate your loved one going home to be with the Lord, where they will walk streets paved with solid gold and claim the many mansions their heavenly Father or Momma or Grandma has stored up for them.

2. When we learn of a death, we often ask, "Who got the body?" or "Who did the body?"—both of which mean "Which funeral home has the deceased person's body?" Though such a question may seem trivial or intrusive, the name of the funeral home that will prepare the deceased for their home-going communicates important information. Many funeral homes have their signature strengths. Some give the deceased great French manicures. Others give their clients life-like smiles. Or the funeral director always quotes John Donne's "For Whom the Bell Tolls" during the service. Some funeral homes do great makeup on Black people, or impressive reconstructive work so families can have the open-casket homegoing of their dreams. And then there are those funeral homes that specialize in the most tricked-out, deluxe home-goings: caskets shaped like cars; the deceased standing up

with shades on; horse-drawn carriages carrying the caskets and doves being released into the air. Knowing the name of the funeral home helps set the attendees' expectations. We like to know what we're walking into. "Who got the body?" is the homegoing equivalent of "Who all gon' be there?"

3. Homegoings are a multi-hour production. The order of service contains many parts: the pre-service viewing of the body; prayer; A and B choir selections (with a bonus song) and solos; scripture readings; remarks by the attendees; the reading of the obituary, cards, and acknowledgments; the eulogy; the altar call; another viewing with the choir singing in the background; and the repast. While most homegoings are not all-day affairs like Aretha Franklin's televised one, you should still eat before you come and bring a snack, like some peppermints and Violet Mints wrapped inside tissue just like your grandma used to do.

4. Black folks love to collect funeral programs. The funeral program is a family heirloom and archaeological artifact. It tells many stories, including those no one dares utter aloud. The obituary—its centerpiece—lists relatives and helps us map out family trees. We look at who is listed as a loved one left behind and who has been excluded, and we rely upon gossip and family lore to fill in the blanks. The obituary tells the story of the Great Migration, rattling off names of the small Southern towns and ghosts from which our ancestors fled; and the destinations, opportunities, and troubles they found elsewhere. We see the name of the deceased person's church listed and realize our family has attended that church since our great-great-grandparents were children. The funeral program's importance is why people who aren't going to the

homegoing will yell out, "Bring me a program!" as if you're headed to a concert or Broadway play. Therefore, it must be a work of art, complete with lots of pictures, poems, and an obituary that includes enough details to serve as required reading in an African American history class. For generations to come, the funeral program will live on in drawers and china cabinets and media storage units and on mirrors across this land. Decades from now, someone will look at it and wonder, *Who was this person? How are they related to me? Why do we still have this?* At some point, everyone will be tasked with planning their own loved ones' homegoings. They, too, will ask questions. *What songs should we sing? What scriptures did they read at Ma'Dear's homegoing? What were Pop-Pop's parents' names?* They will look to their collection of funeral programs as a roadmap and historical source. So, be a Good Samaritan and grab an extra program or two. But don't get mad if the usher sucks her teeth and looks at you sideways. Funeral programs ain't cheap.

5. The deceased must be casket sharp. But "casket sharp" is in the eye of the deceased—not the living beholder. The homegoing's purpose is to honor the life of the deceased, not to subject them to your fashion fantasies and fetishes. Dress your loved one as they dressed in life, not as you had always wished they would look. If she always wore cornrows and baggy jeans while living, do not dress her in a frilly pink suit with a press and curl. If he never owned a suit or hard-soled shoes, do not show up to the funeral home with an outfit from a Stacy Adams store. If you do, we will gossip about your poor choices after the homegoing and repast. *They know good and well she ain't never dressed that way when she was alive. Now, why they do him like that? What happened to*

her hair? If the deceased always showed up to church looking like she was auditioning for a spot on *The Real Housewives of the Fire and Brimstone Church of God in Christ on the Hill,* then you know her final outfit must consist of a fancy hat and a suit with rhinestones and lots of sparkly, glittery beads. If the brotha was on the deacon board, let him go on to glory, wearing his three-piece suit. Allow the deceased to show out in death as they showed out in life. Whatever their thing was, honor it.

6. Every homegoing needs an officiant. The officiant is both emcee and hype man. Anyone can serve in this role: a minister or church member, a family member, or that person who seems to always speak at everyone's homegoing as if they're a professional homegoing spokesperson. The officiant must strike the right balance between being solemn, compassionate, and celebratory. They must be charismatic and lively, like an award show host or a DJ at the club. Though it would be helpful if the officiant were well-versed in the panoply of names whose spellings do not match their pronunciations, or at least familiar enough with the deceased person's family to improvise, this skill is not necessary. If they can keep the crowd jumpin' and praisin' the Lord, no one will care that they butchered every name in the obituary. Equally important as persona are time management skills. The officiant must be firm, aggressive even, in moving attendees along who do not adhere to the three-minute time limit for giving remarks. This may require standing up and saying *God bless ya, brotha* or *We thank God for ya, sista* with an air of finality in their voice. In such instances, the organist should stop playing because nothing gets Black church folks going like good shoutin' music or a call-and-response duet with the organ. If the

speaker doesn't take the hint, the officiant must be willing to make an announcement reminding everyone to stay within the time limits. Otherwise, the cemetery will be closed and the food at the repast will be cold by the time we finish listening to everyone's trial sermon. Lastly, the officiant must realize that even the most meticulously planned order of service can go awry. They must be able to handle conflict and melodrama as they arise. The officiant must know when to intervene and when to just roll with it. The person who gets up and tells all the attendees how much they hated their dead momma? Everybody grieves differently. Just let the Lord use them. They might encourage someone to be a better person, so their own loved ones won't put them on blast when they're dead and gone. That one person who sounds like a battered crow, but insists on singing "His Eye Is on the Sparrow"? As the first line of the song goes, why should they feel discouraged? After all, the Bible commands, "Let everything that hath breath praise ye the Lord." Just rolling with it may mean patting someone on the back as they sob or speak their truth. Or, as everything implodes, it could entail standing by silently with a pensive expression on their face and a *WTF!* in their heart.

7. Black folks talk a lot at homegoings. We never adhere to the rule to keep remarks to three minutes. In this time, you will learn everything you never knew to ask: how you're related to someone; how your godmother or play-aunt met your family; the fact that almost every elderly Black woman you know has worked as a domestic for white folks at some point in her life; the existence of the deceased person's other children and spouses no one knew about. The list of revelations goes on. Just sit back and wave your handkerchief or fan yourself

with your program. Let the grieving oversharers pay homage and mourn in their own way.

8. The song selections at a homegoing will cause even the most stoic person's heart to flutter and eyes to twitch. There is a canon of gospel songs most Black folks know, or can at least mumble along to, even if we haven't been to church since Jesus was a baby. These songs are second nature to us, like knowing the 23rd Psalm or the "Our Father" prayer. There will always be a soloist on hand whose voice is so beautiful, they leave you in a catatonic state as rivers of saltwater stream down your face, but you don't need to have such an effect on others to sing at a homegoing. All that matters is that you dig deep down into the bowels of your soul and belt out all your sorrows and those of your ancestors, too. The soloist, choir, and congregation will sing at least a few of these songs: "Amazing Grace," "His Eye Is on the Sparrow," "I'll Fly Away," "Going Up the Yonder," "Soon and Very Soon," "When We All Get to Heaven," "I Won't Complain," "When I See Jesus," "Walkin' Up the King's Highway," and "Great Gettin' Up Morning."

9. The altar call at a homegoing is one of the most effective ways to guilt-trip folks into coming to Jesus. First, the preacher baits you with a good Bible verse, like Mark 8:36: "For what shall it profit a man, if he shall gain the whole world, and lose his own soul?" Then they hook you by contrasting the deceased person's good virtues with your own moral bankruptcy. "When she pulls up to the pearly gates of heaven, the Lord will say, 'Well done, my good and faithful servant.' What will the Lord say to you? Will He even know who you are? Is your name written in the Lamb's Book of Life?" Or the

preacher will say, "His crown has already been bought and paid for. What about yours? Is it still on layaway?" Finally, the preacher snatches your heart right out of your chest with one last question: "Don't you wanna see your loved one again?" Of course, you do. Before you know it, you've glided to the front of the church, snot and tears staining your face, and you pray, repeat after the preacher (*Father, forgive me for all my sins*), and accept Jesus Christ as your Lord and personal savior.

10. The repast is an opportunity for attendees to reminisce about the deceased, catch up with folks they haven't seen in years, and comfort the family—all over some good food after the homegoing. It can take place in the church's fellowship hall or dining room, the funeral home, or someone's house. But you can't eat everybody's cooking, otherwise we'd all end up in the hospital or six feet under. Some folks should only be assigned to fix plates on the food line or hand out ice and drinks, so only bring food to the repast if you're asked to. If you haven't been given a job, just sit down and eat yo' mac and cheese and collard greens. The family thanks you in advance for your kind consideration.

11. Black folks love pomp and circumstance. We take special care with even the smallest details of a homegoing. Her hands crossed atop a Bible the same color as her outfit. Flowers whose colors match the accent colors on the casket. A nameplate against the casket's lid whose design is the same as that of the prayer cards. Someone to sing their favorite songs. Special instructions to the minister giving the eulogy. *He was from the Holiness Church and liked that loud preaching, so make sure you holla a bit.* Perfectly curated services, seating

arrangements, family processions, and drives through the old neighborhood on the way to the cemetery. A homegoing is the last loving act we'll be able to perform for our dearly departed; the last party we'll be able to throw in their honor. Make it a wonderful send-off, a going-home celebration to remember. This is how we mourn our dead.

4

Running Out of Time

There are two times when families are most likely to show the entire circumference of their asses: in sickness and in death. It is during these times that deeply rooted rivalries and resentments come crashing towards the surface. Family members tussle for information, decision-making power, and assets. Their masks of civility disintegrate to dust. My family was no different. But sometimes you have to leave drama right where you find it.

When I arrived at the intensive care unit, three of Granny's doctors were waiting for me outside her room. I approached slowly, fearing what the solemn looks on their faces might mean. I had previously watched one of them, a man with a thick Latin American accent and large, round piercing gray eyes, rush into Granny's room to administer epinephrine to increase her heart rate. Another, a short, bespectacled woman with a comforting voice, had called me to obtain permission to intubate Granny when she was first admitted. Now she spoke on the group's behalf.

"Your mother keeps calling here," she said. Her tone had changed from its usual friendliness to cold annoyance. "We can't take care of your grandmother *and* all the other patients on the unit *and* talk to your mother every five minutes," the doctor continued.

I was relieved that Granny's condition had not worsened but the last thing I wanted was for her, or any other patient's, care to suffer because of my mother's antics.

"We told your mother she should speak to you, but she said she didn't want to. What's going on?"

I'm usually reluctant to share the details of my estranged relationship with my mother. One question will lead to another, which will then lead to a case study in dysfunction. But Granny's doctors were visibly frustrated. More importantly, I didn't want them to think my mother was authorized to give instructions about Granny's care—something she had never done. So, I explained: My mother didn't live in New York and hadn't seen Granny in several years. I had lived with Granny my entire life. I was her caregiver.

"Well, you're the one we see every day. If your mother cared so much, she'd be up here," the doctor replied. As if on cue, the phone rang and she answered it. "It's her."

I took the receiver from her. "Hello."

"Why didn't you tell me they put Momma in a nursing home?" my mother demanded. *Put Momma in a nursing home*. It was something my family didn't do—even when Auntie Annie Lou, Granny's mother's sister, developed Alzheimer's. *Put Momma in a nursing home*. Something I had vowed never to do, especially after working in one during my last two summers of high school.

I had chosen the nursing home assignment through New York City's Summer Youth Employment Program because I wanted to become an infectious disease specialist. The summer after my junior year, I worked at the clerk's station on the AIDS hospice unit. The following summer, I made the switch to the executive director's office. I spent my days answering telephones, assembling patient charts, filing, and performing other office tasks. Like most people, I originally associated nursing homes with the elderly, but it was the young, thin residents suffering from wasting syndrome on the AIDS unit who instilled a fear of nursing homes in me. The young residents were so close in age to us interns that our supervisor reminded a group of girls that they could not date or befriend the residents. Many of them reminded me of the children in those commercials that urged viewers to donate money to feed starving children in Africa. Nursing homes were where people went to die—alone. Despite patients being surrounded by staff and each other, visits from family were rare.

To this day, when I visit a nursing home, a heavy sadness and loneliness takes over. The smells, the helplessness of the residents, their isolation from the outside world, unmanageable illnesses, and impending death always weigh on me. About a year before Granny's death, my then-boyfriend and I visited his elderly godfather in a nursing home. I smiled my way through a greeting when we walked into his room, then looked on blankly as the two of them spoke.

"What's wrong?" my boyfriend eventually asked me.

"Nothing," I whispered. My smile had come undone and been replaced by a caul of grief for what had been and what was to come. I wondered how much longer his godfather would live. I thought the same thing about Granny.

I can't seem to escape these places. I live near a nursing home now. Whenever I pass it, I look up at its windows and imagine the lives and days of its residents. I say a prayer whenever I see an ambulance parked at the entrance. I wonder if I will someday move the short distance from my current apartment to one of its rooms.

When a family member suggested I move Granny from our home in New York to a nursing home in Florida so the rest of the family could see her more often, I ignored the idea. There was no way I was going to move Granny to a state she had not lived in since her twenties, to live in a nursing home that family members would probably only visit on holidays and birthdays. Not to mention that I had never lived in Florida and had no intention of moving there any time soon. I wanted Granny to age in place, as the experts say. To stay in her home with me—the person best suited to make sure she was properly loved and cared for.

My mother's question echoed in my mind.

Why didn't you tell me they put Momma in a nursing home?

Because my mother wasn't responsible enough to change the hanging bags of liquid food and the feeding tube inserted into Granny's abdomen. My mother could not be counted on to transport Granny to feeding therapy so she could relearn to swallow. Nor could she contribute money to pay for nurses to come to our home and perform these tasks. She couldn't even keep a working phone to receive regular updates about Granny. My mother couldn't help at a time when I felt helpless.

Her question felt like an indictment of me and my decision—the decision the hospital had made and I had no choice but to consent to. I didn't bother giving my mother the details of the who or how or why. There was no point. She would only end up disappearing again. I was furious.

Why didn't you tell me they put Momma in a nursing home?

"Tell you for what?" I responded. "What would you have done?"

"Well, she's my mother," she yelled.

"Well, I'm the one who has been taking care of your mother." Drug-addicted prodigal daughters do not get to question decisions about the lives that continue without them.

The phone clicked, followed by a dial tone.

I hung up and turned around. Granny's doctors were staring at me. The looks on their faces told me they'd overheard the entire conversation. So much for avoiding the embarrassment of looking a hot ghetto mess in front of these white folks. I smiled awkwardly, said, "I'm so sorry," and headed to Granny's room.

Granny used to send me to Florida during the summers and come get me right before school started back up in the fall. I'd stay with either

her older sister Jennye, or her younger sister Lilla, who we called Aunt Lil. Aunt Lil was the executive director of the local YWCA's daycare center. Every morning, my brother, cousins, and I would go to work with her. We'd perform various jobs, like washing dishes, serving the kids food, reading to them, or watching them as they played outside. Whenever we had kitchen duty, we'd throw water on each other or turn up the radio and sing along to songs like Troop's "Spread My Wings," H-Town's "Knockin' Da Boots," and Mariah Carey's "Vision of Love."

Although my mother was often MIA during my summer visits, she sometimes stopped by the Y for food or money. On one of her visits, she was frailer than usual. Her limbs looked like thin sticks. Black keloid-like sores covered her arms and the back of her neck. She once told me she'd gotten the sores because of the filth she often lived in.

"Sometimes I be so shame to come around the family cus of how I look," she said.

I still loved my mother—through her sores and emaciation and disappearing acts.

That day at the Y, she wanted to sleep. I wanted to be next to her, so I followed her to a dark room near the front of the building. We laid together on a small, child's cot—my mother with her back against the wall, spooning me as I lay facing the doorway across from us.

"Don't leave while I'm sleeping," I told her.

"I won't," she promised.

When I awoke, she was gone.

When I was a little girl, my mother gave Aunt Jennye a necklace and ring to hold for me until I turned eighteen.

"You know I'll sell 'em for some drugs if I keep 'em," she'd told Aunt Jennye.

The necklace was a short, thick gold rope. The gold ring had an apple jade stone in the center with a small diamond on each side.

Aunt Jennye kept her promise. She wore the necklace every day, no matter what outfit she had on. She put the ring away for safe-keeping. When she died during my senior year of high school, her husband Uncle Roosevelt removed the necklace from her neck so that he could give it to me. He also gave me the ring, which my mother had described but I'd never seen. For years, I wrapped pieces of tape on each side of the ring so that it would fit snugly on my finger. Nearly twenty-five years after Aunt Jennye's death, I still have the jewelry. They are reminders that my mother, in a sober moment of lucidity, devised a way to overcome her own urges so that I could have something valuable when I was older. Sometimes the most loving thing a mother can do is let go.

About three years before my mother hung up on me as I stood outside Granny's hospital room, my neighbor Pat called to tell me Granny had walked two doors down to her house earlier that day, after Granny's home attendant's shift had ended.

"She was crying and talking about how your mother wanted to move in," Pat explained. "She said you were gonna move out, and that she didn't want your mother to come live with her."

Granny was in the early stages of Alzheimer's disease. She had forgotten all about her conversation with Pat by the time I got home from work and didn't mention it to me.

It was true that my mother had asked to come live with us. She was about to be discharged from a prison work release program in Florida and would need somewhere to live.

"I can help you take care of Momma," my mother would tell me.

I was overwhelmed with the responsibilities of caring for Granny and working full time and initially thought this was a good idea. It would be a chance for all three of us to start over. I was excited about the prospect of finally having the mother-daughter relationship I had always wanted. We talked about our plans, including my mother accompanying me to a gynecology appointment I kept putting off. Granny also held on to dreams of starting over with my mother—her daughter. She too wanted a second chance. It had the makings of a perfect *New York Times* bestseller.

Running Out of Time

> This novel follows three generations of women reunited by the matriarch's illness. When Charlotte returns home to New York after nearly thirty years to help care for her mother, who has Alzheimer's disease, the three Smith women begin a journey of forgiveness and acceptance. They heal old wounds, repair broken bonds, and break the cycle of secrets. This exploration of mother-daughter relationships lays bare the human frailties that connect us all.

Unfortunately, our lives were not a beach read or Lifetime movie. The truth is my mother was an addict.

"But I haven't used drugs since I went to prison," she would say to convince me that she'd remain sober and reliable. Her delusional optimism reminded me of my time as a judicial law clerk for a family court judge right after I graduated from law school. Women would plead with my judge to lift their restraining orders because their husbands/boyfriends/children's fathers hadn't beat them while the order was active. "He hasn't hit you because I ordered him to stay away from you," my judge would reply in a strained, high-pitched voice that signaled her frustration and fear for the women's safety.

Granny shared my mother's faith in the improbable. Their sporadic calls, and visits when we went to Florida, were always laced with a mix of Granny's heartbreak, disappointment, and optimism. She'd pray for my mother and tell her, "You're my only chile." Granny believed the Bible's promise that "the prayers of the righteous availeth much." She never lost hope that God would one day deliver my mother from her drug addiction.

I knew how this story would turn out: I'd end up chasing down stolen money, household items, and identities if I allowed my mother to come live with us. My mother's rap sheet and drug history were almost as old as me. Most of her crimes had been motivated by her need to get money for drugs. She'd gone through numerous drug rehab programs, only to relapse. My family had long stopped allowing my mother to live with them, for fear that she would steal from them. And no one wanted a parade of addicts and dealers traipsing through their house all day. Not to mention that my Brooklyn neighborhood had its fair share of drug dealers, some of whom I'd grown up with. It would take more than wishful thinking about what could have been, but never was, to keep my mother clean. And I had Granny to worry about. I had too much to lose.

"If you let her move in, I'm moving out," I told Granny. I had no intentions of following through with my threat, but I thought it would get her to give up her fantasy of a three-generation reunion. Granny continued telling my mother she could move in.

After Granny's breakdown at Pat's, I realized it was time to tell my mother no. But first, I told Granny I wouldn't be moving out or allowing my mother to live with us.

"Okay," she said with relief in her voice.

Then I told my mother the news.

"Well, I'm coming anyway. It's Momma's house and she said I can come," she arrogantly responded. I channeled Granny's quiet, righteous indignation and uttered the same warning she had given to the invisible people who lived with us.

"If you show up, I will call the cops on you."

Although the threat never worked for the invisible people, my mother quickly changed course.

She went to live with my brother when she was released. Before showing up at his apartment high, she stopped somewhere and binged for a few days. When she grew tired of struggling to remain sober, she left my brother's front door wide open and drove off in his car. Our tenuous relationship began to crumble with that single decision. It was a clear declaration: I choose Granny over you. I choose myself over you. But I don't regret my choice. Drug addicts aren't reliable, even when they love you. They can't be counted on to show up and stay put. You can't put your hopes and dreams and grandmothers in their hands.

My mother once asked me what I wanted for Christmas. "A curling iron," I replied. I needed the right tools to create the hairstyles my older cousins and all the cool girls at school wore.

I was disappointed when I realized none of the boxes wrapped in reds and greens and snowflakes under the Christmas tree in Florida contained my curling iron, but I wasn't surprised. My mother had always been consistent in her absence. Luckily, Aunt Jennye, Aunt Chris, and the rest of my family always got carried away with their holiday shopping and made sure I had plenty of presents. Cabbage Patch Kids, Rainbow Bright, and My Kid Sister dolls. Pretty clothes from JCPenney, Lord & Taylor, Burdines, and Jacobson's. A Sega Genesis or a Gameboy. Even when Granny and I spent Christmases in New York, my aunts mailed gifts that arrived early, giving me weeks to guess what was in the various sized boxes. I was used to not seeing my mother or receiving gifts from her during the holidays, but she would at least call. That year, she didn't.

"I'm sorry I didn't call you on Christmas," she told me when she called a few days later. "A John robbed me and beat me up real bad."

Although I was in elementary school, I knew what a "John" was and what my mother did with Johns. I'd always lived with the fact of my mother's addiction. I wasn't shocked that she had sex with men for money. She even referred to her vagina as her "pocketbook." Have sex with men for money. Use money to buy drugs. Repeat. Even as a child, I understood the cycle.

I did not judge my mother. I prayed for divine intervention instead. I'd go to the altar at church on Sunday mornings and ask my pastor to pray for her healing. I wrote letters to God asking Him to make her stop using drugs. Perhaps I was too young to question other people's life choices. Too young to know, or assume, people could choose differently. All I knew was that a man had hurt my mother. On Christmas day. In a car on the side of the road. He could have killed her. Taken her away from me forever. Destroyed all hope that God would one day answer my prayers.

A few days after the phone confrontation with my mother at the hospital, I called her so she could talk to Granny. Although the respirator tubes prevented Granny from speaking, she could at least hear her daughter's voice. I held the phone to Granny's ear for several moments. When I removed it, thinking my mother had finished talking, Granny frowned and looked up at me with furrowed eyebrows. It was the same piercing look she used to give me as a little girl whenever I misbehaved. It was the same look she gave the nurses when they woke her at night to check her vitals or take blood. Not realizing I was now on the phone, my mother kept talking.

"Momma, I'm sorry for not being the daughter I should have been," she said. I returned the phone to Granny's ear. Granny listened attentively, soaking up her only child's voice for the last time.

When we had argued, I thought I heard indignation and entitlement and judgment in my mother's voice. Maybe I did. But I think

I also heard panic. Time was running out. Time to fix her life before Granny closed her eyes. Time to make amends for her mistakes. Time to make her momma proud. For her to realize time had already run out must have been a hard truth to face.

My mother was in jail when I started high school. She wrote this letter to Granny:

September 10, 1992

Dear Mom,

How was Jodi's first day of school? Tell her I love her very much. I will be going to court soon. Pray for me. Mom, please write me okay. Tell Jodi the truth please. I am okay.

The truth was that my mother was in jail awaiting trial, although I do not remember the offense for which she had been arrested. Granny always told me the truth, but I learned to hide it from others.

In the fall of 1992, I began my freshman year of high school at Brooklyn Technical High School of Science and Engineering, a specialized school in New York City with an entrance exam. Its multicultural student body was much more diverse than those of the elementary and junior high schools I'd attended in East New York and Brownsville, where most of the students were Black and Hispanic, from poor or working-class families, and lived in the communities in which the schools were located. Among my elementary and junior high classmates, having a parent or family member who was addicted to drugs or who had been in jail wasn't uncommon. I'd never felt ashamed about discussing my mother.

That changed in high school. When my new classmates asked me why I lived with Granny instead of my parents, I lied and said my mother was attending pharmacy school in Florida. Given her history of using illegal pharmaceuticals, pharmacy school was the quickest and most plausible story I could come up with. The fact that my mother would've been thirty-two years old at the time is a minor detail that had escaped my attention. (I did not yet know about the concept of the "non-traditional student," who was typically older or changing careers.) No one ever questioned me beyond that or asked about my father. It's just as well. I hadn't come up with a story to explain his absence.

As time went on, everyone forgot about my mother's whereabouts and focused on Granny, who once picked up the phone and interrupted my conversation to tell my classmate to stop asking me for all the answers to our homework assignments. Who came to every parent-teacher night and demanded that I be home from school by 3:30 PM every day—exactly thirty minutes after school let out. I had to beg her to let me participate in extracurricular activities like the gospel choir, a poetry workshop in the city, and NSBE, Jr. (the high school division of the National Society of Black Engineers).

By the time I graduated, I was more comfortable with the truth. Thinking about the kind of future I wanted—one that was not like my mother's life of addiction—required that I be honest about her situation. It also helped that, whether they talked openly about their home life or not, many of my classmates did not come from "perfect" families with a mother, father, siblings, and pets all under one roof either. By the time I was in college, I was done hiding. During my graduation, when I told my classmates, "My mother is on vacation," they understood that she was in jail. Some of them had relatives who'd taken the same trip.

When Granny passed away, I decided that she'd have two funerals—one in New York, where we lived, and the other in Florida, where she was born and most of our family lived. She'd be laid to rest in a grave with her younger sister Lilla, not far from their mother's grave and the mausoleum that held their sister Jennye. Granny would take one final flight, this time in her pink-and-white casket in the belly of the plane.

"When is Momma's body getting here?" my mother asked me several days after Granny's death. She did not preface her question with "Hello" or "How are you?"

In the chasm between my mother's spoken and unspoken words lay the realization that she would not comfort me. I could not share my grief with her; nor would she share her grief with me.

My mother had a habit of withholding words in order to hurt me. Like the time she called our house on my birthday and only said, "Lemme speak to Momma." Her tone, abrupt with a hint of laughter, suggested that she had intentionally refused to wish me happy birthday. She was most likely still upset because I had told her she could not come live with Granny and me. Or maybe because I had refused to send her money. I was in my late twenties or early thirties, yet the sting of her unspoken words was especially sharp. By then, Granny no longer remembered my birthday.

The little girl in me wanted to ask my mother, *Did you forget? It's my birthday!* No matter how old we are, everyone wants their mother to acknowledge them. To see them. My mother wishing me a happy birthday would have been the same as her saying, "You matter to me. Your existence is worth celebrating." The adult me gave the phone to Granny without further conversation. I did not give my mother the satisfaction of knowing she had hurt me.

And when my mother called to find out when Granny would make her final trip home, I did not acknowledge her failure to acknowledge me. I did not discuss the celebratory atmosphere of Granny's New York homegoing or mention that the hospital chaplain, who had visited and prayed for Granny several times before she died, pulled me up to dance during the service because Granny loved a good Pentecostal holy dance. We did not marvel at the fact that we shared the same godmother, who had christened us both as children, more than twenty years apart, and that she had attended Granny's homegoing. We did not laugh about the fact that I had placed a tiara atop Granny's head instead of a church lady hat, because she wore a tiara during her birthday party every year and loved being treated like a queen. Nor did we reminisce about Granny's holy roller ways and talk about how much she would have loved all the hollerin' and singing and speaking in tongues during her homegoing. We did not swap happy memories or tears. I knew then that we would not mourn the loss of our mother together.

The only birthday card I remember ever receiving from my mother is the one she sent me from jail for my fourteenth birthday, a few weeks after I started high school in 1992. She had made it herself by folding a piece of white paper in half. On the front, she used a black pen to draw an intricate, calligraphy-like rose with thorns. She did not color it in, but drew a red ribbon wrapped around the white rose. Beside it, she wrote in big graffiti letters, "Happy 14th Birthday Jodi." She wrote a message for me on the inside.

Jodi,

I wish I could be with you on your special day. You will be in my thoughts and prayers. Happy Birthday!

Love Ya,
Your Mother

That birthday card hung on my bedroom wall until I was thirty-two years old. When I was ready to take it down, I took a picture of it and saved it on my phone. But sometimes I take the three-dimensional card out to remember the imperfect love of the woman whose hands crafted it.

When I arrived in Florida for Granny's second funeral and burial, Uncle Bill—Granny's twin brother—told me that my mother had called the funeral home the day before my arrival and asked whether there was any insurance money. The funeral director refused to give her any information.

"But I'm her daughter," my mother told him. This was always her refrain, her shield and sword, as if it relayed anything other than a biological relationship.

"I understand, but your uncle made all of the arrangements," the funeral director replied. "You should speak to him."

My mother never called Uncle Bill. If there had been insurance money, I don't know why she'd think she was entitled to it. I don't know why she thought she could just waltz into the funeral home where her dead mother lay and demand an accounting.

"She said she gon' kill you," Aunt Chris told me. "What is it with you two? I've never seen a mother and daughter so at odds." I didn't understand the source of my mother's venom because we'd never had a physical altercation. I took the phone from Aunt Chris when my mother later called the house.

"Is there something you need to say to me?" I asked my mother.

"No," she answered in a tone that said she did, but thought it wiser to hold her tongue.

I kept my distance from my mother and even had a bodyguard at the funeral. An older cousin, who'd grown up with my mother, stayed by my side in case she tried anything.

At the funeral chapel, I sat near the end of the pew closest to the wall, sandwiched between my bodyguard cousin and another family member, with Uncle Bill and Aunt Chris at the other end. Although I generally felt like I was on my own in life, I felt safe and enveloped in love at Granny's homegoing. My mother sat across the aisle from Aunt Chris and Uncle Bill, in a pew with my father and four younger siblings. My parents had not lived together since I was an infant, and my father subsequently had two daughters and two sons with another woman, but he and my mother were still friends. And they were legally married. I was thirty-two years old at the time, twenty-one years older than the youngest of my siblings. Granny wasn't their biological grandmother and they'd only met her a handful of times, but they still called her "Granny Poo," the same pet name I'd used for her. Whenever my father spoke to Granny, which was rare, he ended the conversation with, "Ms. McKinney, thank you for raising Jodi." He expressed his gratitude one last time by helping to carry her casket from the chapel to the hearse waiting outside.

Towards the end of the service, my mother went up to Granny's casket and looked down at her.

"She looks so peaceful," my mother said as she cried loudly enough for everyone to hear and stroked Granny's lace-gloved hands. I wanted to go up and see Granny one last time, but I didn't move. I didn't want to risk my mother acting a plumb fool. I also didn't want to intrude on her final moments with her mother. She hadn't seen Granny in several years. I had already spent time with Granny the day before, when my cousin and uncle drove me straight from the airport to the funeral home. So I watched until my mother returned to her seat. I watched as the funeral director handed me Granny's tiara and the Bible all the guests had signed. I watched as he turned the casket crank and lowered Granny's head further into her casket until she disappeared.

In January of 1996, I anxiously awaited an early admissions decision from Barnard College. The stakes were high. I'd considered applying to Smith, Wells, and Spelman (also all-women's colleges), but only actually applied to one other school—New York University. I'd been obsessed with attending Barnard since my junior year of high school and planned to major in biology and be on a pre-med track. I wanted to bask in all the brilliance and flyness of other women, in an environment where it was cool for girls to be nerds. By applying early decision, I committed to attending if accepted.

When the time came, Granny and I were visiting family in Florida and staying at Aunt Lil's. My mother had stopped by. It was just the three of us. Finally, no longer able to stand the suspense, I called Barnard to see if they'd made a decision. They had: I'd been accepted. I was going to the feminist liberation school of my dreams.

"Thank you, Jesus," Granny said and started clapping. Jesus had heard her prayers.

My mother ran out of the bathroom, still naked, and hugged me.

"My daughter got into college!" she kept yelling, as she jumped up and down. I'd never seen her so joyful and animated.

"Put some clothes on," Granny admonished my mother in between her prayers of thanksgiving.

I wonder if Granny and my mother acted out a similar scene years earlier when they found out my mother had received a four-year scholarship to attend Bethune-Cookman College. My mother had planned to major in criminal justice. She had instead fallen onto the merry-go-round of drug addiction and the criminal justice system.

"Lemme call your daddy and tell him the news," my mother said.

I had not seen my father in years. I was surprised that she still kept in touch with him. It was then that I learned he had been living, not in Virginia as I'd previously thought, but in New Jersey—one state over from me. *If he didn't think enough of me to contact or see me after moving so close, I doubt he cares about my good news*, I thought. My mother called the most recent number she had for him. I don't remember if we reached my father that day. It didn't matter. That moment was glorious. Granny, my mother, and I were together and happy and excited about the future.

"Jodi," my mother called out to me at the cemetery after Granny's burial. She clumsily ran towards me, her shoes sinking into the soft dirt and grass with each step. My heart sped up. This was it. My mother and I were going to throw down in the cemetery like two mean girls on a reality TV show.

As my mother got closer, she stretched out her arms. With a puzzled look on my face, I backed up.

She continued towards me.

When she was finally close enough to grab me, she wrapped her arms around me and laid her face on my chest. Her affection was awkward and unexpected.

"I'm sorry," she said through tears. "I love you."

"Okay," I replied. My cousin led me away to a car nearby.

A year or so after Granny's death, I put our home on the market. It had become too dark and too sad and too lonely without her. My real estate agent called one day to tell me she'd received a call from an agent in New Orleans. According to the New Orleans agent, my mother claimed that Granny had just died and left her $50,000. My mother had hired the New Orleans agent to sell Granny's house in Brooklyn, New York.

I was livid. I sent friends a rapid succession of profanity-filled text messages, while trying to explain to my newly minted real estate agent why my mother would lie about a cash inheritance that didn't exist and attempt to sell a home she didn't own. The age-old tale of death and drama. My anger—and hurt—intensified as the weight of what my mother had attempted to do set in. Without so much as a mention or care, she had planned to kick me out of the home I'd lived in my entire life—one she had not visited since I was an infant more than thirty years earlier. Although I had already intended to sell *my* home, my mother did not know that when she walked into the New Orleans realtor's office.

I'd like to think my mother's callous, hateful actions were the desperate and impulsive moves of a crack addict not graced with all her good senses. But they hurt just the same. I made sure to keep an even greater distance from her after house-gate. I did not confront her about what she had tried to do; nor did she bring it up. We didn't talk for several years. When I eventually sold my home and moved, I did not give her my address. I threatened to stop speaking to other family members if they shared my contact information with her. When I got a new job, I didn't update my LinkedIn profile and only shared the name of my new employer with a small group of coworkers. I also warned them to never give her any information if she called. You don't give folks a second chance to hurt you, not even your own mother.

Five years after Granny's death, my brother and Aunt Chris told me my mother had breast cancer and would need to have a mastectomy.

"You should come," Aunt Chris told me.

Always dramatic, my mother asked me, "Am I going to see you before I die?"

"Chile, I don't know," I responded. I hadn't seen or spoken to her since Granny's funeral years earlier. I didn't know how much time she had left—how much time we had left. Time had run out for her and Granny, so I went to see her.

I spent about a week in Florida after I found out about my mother's diagnosis. She and I spent a lot of time together during that Florida trip.

"She talks about you all the time," her neighbor Sharon told me as the three of us stood in front of Sharon's apartment. My mother wasn't familiar with the latest happenings in my life because we had not spoken in years. But judging by my mother's wide, gap-toothed smile, I assumed she had repeated with pride the refrain often used by Granny and others in my family whenever they introduced me or talked about me to others: *Jodi's a lawyer.* Although neither of my parents had raised me, I always allowed them to indulge in their bragging sessions uninterrupted. No matter how old we get, no matter how spotty our parents' records are, all children want our parents to see and be proud of us.

"We need to talk," my mother told me one day at Uncle Bill and Aunt Chris's house. We walked out of the house and settled into the chairs on the porch. Aunt Chris followed us and remained at the door.

"Close the door, ma'am," I told Aunt Chris.

"Yeah, we gotta talk," my mother chimed in.

Aunt Chris closed the door slowly and retreated to the window behind us, peeking from behind the curtains before finally disappearing, most likely to update Uncle Bill about the peace accord happening in front of their house.

"I'm sorry for not being there for you. For everything," my mother told me.

I had long forgiven her for not being the mother I needed her to be. Because of Granny, I had never been motherless or unloved. But since she was in the mood for apologies, it was the perfect time to make her address every grievance I could think of.

"Are you also sorry for trying to sell my house?" I asked her.

She let out a short, high-pitched laugh and threw her head back. It was a laugh of surprise that yelled, *Damn, she caught me red-handed and had the balls to call me out to my face.*

"Yeah, I am," she replied.

"Why would you do that?"

"Because I didn't get anything when Aunt Lil and Aunt Jennye died, and I didn't get anything from the Big House."

The "Big House" was the Florida home Granny and her siblings Jennye, Lilla, and Bill had grown up in. Granny's younger sister Lilla was the only sibling who continued living there after their mother and stepfather died. After Aunt Lil passed away, different family members moved in and out of the Big House. It remained in the family, the source of hurt feelings over who should own it, profit from it, and live in it.

"And the same thing happened with Momma," she continued. "I didn't get anything when she died either."

I didn't press the issue any further. I did not tell my mother she had no right to take what wasn't hers. I did not tell my mother she had no right to covet or mourn a home that had never been more than a layover stop for her more than thirty years ago. None of it mattered now.

We talked for a while longer—about our family, about ourselves, about things she'd never told anyone.

"Now that I've seen you, I'm ready to die," my mother said to me.

My mother was hospitalized the day before I returned to New York. Her friends Mason and Janice, a couple bound together by love and drug addiction, visited while I was at the hospital. Observing my mother's friendships over the years taught me there is no greater loyalty than that between drug addicts. I could not tell if Mason looked significantly older than Janice because he was actually older or because his bald head and thin frame ravaged by cancer and drugs had prematurely aged him. Janice kept trying to convince my mother to request a prescription for pain medication in both the patch and pill form. "She think she slick. I know she be stealin' Mason's pain meds," my mother told me later. The four of us continued talking as we waited for my mother's doctor to return to the room.

"She didn't know if you was gonna come," Janice told me. "Forgive her. She loves you and you only get one mother."

I've always had two mothers—the one who birthed me and the one who raised me. After Granny's death, I've had to wrestle with what it means to lose one mother while reckoning with the mother that's still here. I had thought my Florida trip would be a turning point in my relationship with my mother. That we would be closer and talk frequently. That I would be able to call her for life advice and gossip on the phone with her for hours. After all, sickness and death have a way of shifting one's perspectives and relationships. I had hoped my mother would pick up where Granny left off. But reckoning with the mother left behind meant facing her flaws and limitations. My mother was incapable of being the mother of my childhood fantasies. She could never replace Granny. No one could.

I'm not ready to give my address to my mother or let her come visit me. But she now has my telephone number. She texts me pictures of herself sporting a new wig, a new pair of glasses, or new eyelashes. When we speak, she updates me about the latest family gossip and her life—her latest drug rehab program, the spread of her breast cancer, her dreams to go on a shopping spree in New York and travel to Paris. I listen but usually don't offer many details about my life, because such conversations would take too much time—time we don't have; time that would be wasted. I know it's just a matter of time before my mother will say, "I gotta go. I love you." Just a matter of time before she will leave. Drug addicts aren't reliable, even when they love you.

I was diagnosed with breast cancer in October of 2020—nine years after Granny's death. My mother and I spoke often during my treatment. But even then, her addiction was always lurking. Whenever we didn't speak for an extended time, I knew she was out getting high.

"I got depressed about your diagnosis and mine," she told me after one of her disappearances. Her doctor had recently said her cancer was not responding to the chemo.

Despite our frequent phone calls, my mother also wanted to support me in person.

"I'm gonna come to New York," she told me before my surgery. "I don't want you to have to go through this alone like I did." Any woman would want to hear those comforting words from her mother. But drug addicts aren't reliable, even when they love you.

"I'll be fine. I have friends and neighbors who can help me out." My mother had not been to New York since my birth forty-two years earlier. She had only been clean for a little over a month. She had stage 4 breast cancer that had spread to her bones and liver, and a host of other medical complications. My mother could not help me. She could barely help herself. I quickly spewed out excuses to keep her from coming to New York. *We're in the middle of a pandemic. You'd have to quarantine for two weeks before seeing me. If I have a mastectomy, only one person at a time will be able to visit me in the hospital. We'll both have compromised immune systems. I don't need your COVID germs and you don't need mine.*

"Well, I'm still coming anyway," she told me.

She changed her mind after she was hospitalized and a friend informed her that the number of COVID cases in New York had risen.

"I got mad cus I thought you just didn't want me to come," my mother told me from her hospital bed. "But I guess you were telling the truth."

I had hoped Granny's death would make my mother and me closer. Instead, our own mortality and shared diagnosis had done so. She never gave me the talk about the birds and the bees and menstrual cycles. But she provides motherly counsel about a different coming-of-age journey—one involving mastectomies and lumpectomies, hormone therapy and chemo, treatment side effects and the things doctors don't tell you. She tells me what to expect when I start radiation.

"Radiation burned the shit outta me," she says. "I ain't gon lie. When I saw that scab on my back, I went out and got high and never went back for another treatment."

She shares her recipe for living.

"I can't complain. I have more good days than bad days," she says. "Those days that I'm not tired, bitch, I ride out."

5

The Death of a Jaybird

I.

I'd heard the chirping in my office for days but couldn't figure out where it was coming from. There was a window near my desk and a tree just outside it. Perhaps a bird was nesting nearby. But when I went outside to investigate, the chirping had stopped.

I came back in and alerted my coworker Jim, whose office was right next to mine. Although he also heard the birdsong, he was unable to locate its source. It was time to escalate matters. I marched off to find Marcus, our department's deputy director. The three of us silently placed our ears up against the wall beside my desk. The chirping became louder. "Maybe it's coming from inside the wall," Marcus said. Using scissors, he punched a hole in the sheetrock and peered down into the darkness. "There it is."

A small bird stood wedged between the inner and outer walls. Although it moved around, it didn't flap its little wings. Perhaps it was injured. Or maybe it was exhausted from days of crying out for help and weak from a lack of water and food. I named the bird Little Jimmie, after my coworker Jim, even though we didn't know whether it was male or female. We couldn't get to Little Jimmie right away, so I dropped morsels of my lunch—bread and baked ziti—down to him as my coworkers tore apart the wall and worked to free him.

By the time we lifted Little Jimmie out, he was silent and had stopped moving. I felt guilty because we didn't rescue him in time. Had the ziti and bread killed him? Maybe he had choked, or the meal was too much for his miniature digestive system to handle. Little Jimmie deserved to go out in style. A bird homegoing fit for a king.

I found a small box and placed Little Jimmie inside. Six of my co-workers, including Jim and Marcus, fell into procession and followed Little Jimmie and me outside to the tree in front of my office window. The patch of dirt was too hard for us to dig even a small grave, so instead we stood in a semi-circle around the trash can and eulogized him and prayed for his soul. I held him in his casket.

Little Jimmie was a good bird. Rest in peace, Little Jimmie. Sorry we couldn't save you in time, Little Jimmie.

I gently lowered Little Jimmie's casket into the trash can. We returned to work before our boss had time to wonder where half her employees had gone.

Ìyá mi means "my mother" in Yoruba. The Iyami, also known as "the mothers" or "owners of the bird," are women endowed with spiritual powers that can be used for good or bad. Birds represent the Iyami's spiritual power, also called àṣẹ or Aje, which was given to them by the deity Olodumare. The Iyami gather at night, release their birds from a calabash (or transform into birds themselves), and send them out on a mission or to deliver a message. Once the birds complete the mission, they return to the Iyami and are placed back into their respective calabash. I wonder what message Little Jimmie came to deliver.

II.

Have you ever walked outside and seen random dead birds lying around? Perhaps the mixture of crushed pink organs and feathers was roadkill. Maybe the poor soul was killed by some other inhabitant of the wild—the rural wilderness or the streets of Big City, USA.

Or maybe something else, made more ominous by its invisibility and effect on multiple birds, was responsible. Public health agencies track and test dead birds because they're often the first sign of West Nile Virus activity in an area.[*] Blue jays and crows are the species most likely to die when infected with the virus. Birds that die this way are usually found by themselves, rather than in a group.

In 2012 researchers first observed that jays have homegoings for their dearly departed. When the jays encounter one of their dead, they gather around the body and make calls known as zeeps, scolds, and zeep-scolds to encourage other jays to join them.[†] The birds mourn their dead with much singing, to spread the sad news and announce the service through the avian grapevine. They stop searching for food, sometimes for over a day, in order to call out to each other. Experts believe this behavior may have evolved as a way to warn other birds of possible danger nearby, thereby decreasing the chance of their encountering whatever killed the deceased bird.[‡]

I remember the first time I saw him. I was standing on the porch that night, talking on the phone to my friend Anthony. Suddenly, an animal scurried away from the bowl of food I'd left out for my stray black cat Tweety and jumped up onto the porch's ledge and into our neighbor's yard.

What the fuck was that? I didn't know if it was a cat or small dog, or a rare breed of squirrel or raccoon that had escaped from some-

---

* California West Nile Virus Website, Vector-Borne Disease Section, California Department of Public Health. Accessed May 15, 2023. https://westnile.ca.gov/.

† Rachel Nuwer, "Birds Hold Funerals For Fallen Comrades," *Smithsonian Magazine*, September 3, 2012. Accessed March 23, 2023. https://www.smithsonianmag.com/smart -news/birds-hold-funerals-for-fallen-comrades-24355940/.

‡ Ibid.

body's zoo or wildlife conservation. I could only make out its light-colored coat and long, bushy tail in the dark.

A few days later Granny cried, "Get it away, get it away!" as she peeked out the front door. That's when I saw the mystery animal in daylight for the first time. His white fur was dirty and matted. He had big, bulging eyes, buck teeth, and a mushed-in, flat face. His body was thin and mostly fur. He looked like a Persian cat that had seen better days. I named him Gremlin, after his uncanny appearance to the creatures in the movie. Like them, he looked like he might freak out and run off at the first sign of water.

Gremlin visited us daily.

In all the years we'd lived in our house, we'd never had as much cat action as when Granny developed Alzheimer's disease—as if her illness had brought with it a need for company and something else to focus on besides her waning memory and phantom visitors. Before Gremlin, Tweety was our only porch resident. I named the black cat after the Looney Tunes canary because of his yellow eyes, and because he never meowed. He chirped like a bird instead. I later learned that was because my neighbor James's rottweiler Rocky had caught Tweety and ripped his voice box to shreds. I ignored the commonly held superstition that black cats are bad luck and sometimes let Tweety in the house so that he could be warm. I eventually took Tweety to the vet to get all his shots and moved him inside.

He finally stopped pooping in the tub, but he scared Granny speechless by jumping on her lap and staring at her. I discovered the pair in a stand-off after I heard Granny repeatedly saying "Help," in a monotonous tone. When I approached them, Tweety jumped off her lap and ran upstairs. He hissed at me from his litter house. When I finally picked him up, he dug his claws into my bare thighs and hung on for dear life. I evicted Tweety that night. But I still fed him daily and bought a little outdoor house for him so he could keep warm on our porch in the winter.

Gremlin was much more aggressive than Tweety. He'd eat all the food out of the pan I'd set down for him and Tweety to share. When I placed two pans next to one another, Gremlin still ate out of both. Finally, I placed the pans of food far enough apart for Tweety to have enough time to eat in peace.

Gremlin was quick and slow at the same time. Quick when he wanted to steal food; slow when walking away, as if he was unafraid of the world around him, wanting to underscore his irreverence. Gremlin and his grimacing face grew on me. He could be sweet and mischievous and occasionally he'd let me rub his scrawny sides. I made a game out of dangling my keychain in front of him. He'd climb up onto my legs and grab at the shiny metal.

Small dead birds began materializing on our porch in the mornings. There was nothing else around; there seemed to be no explanation for the deluge of carcasses. Had someone placed them there as part of some sacrificial ritual? Granny and I had once seen an old Black woman walk past our house, mumble some words, and sprinkle a powder onto the ground. We assumed it was goofer dust, a powder used in hoodoo rituals. Anything was possible.

Each time the dead birds appeared, I swept them up, placed them in the trash can, and poured hot water mixed with bleach onto the ground. One morning I found Gremlin eating the remains of one of the dead bird offerings. That's when I realized he was the killer.

How to Dispose of a Dead Bird

1. Make sure the bird is dead before touching or getting too close.

2. Prevent exposure to pets, farm animals, and children.

3. Avoid direct contact with the bird or any fluids coming out of the bird.

4. Be careful of its beak and claws.

5. Wear plastic or latex gloves or use several leak-proof plastic bags as a glove.

6. Place the bird in a double plastic bag and close tightly, making sure the claws or beak do not puncture the bags. For larger birds, or for birds that have extensive trauma, decay, or maggot infestation, insert the bags into a can or pail, then use a shovel to place the bird into the bag-lined container.

7. If examination by the environmental department is likely, place the bird in a cool location or on ice.

8. Bury the remains in a location that will protect both surface water and groundwater from contamination; triple bag the bird and dispose of it in a landfill; or, if in rural or suburban areas far from neighbors, move the bird to an un-mowed, brushy, or wooded area at the edge of your property for natural decomposition.

9. Wash hands thoroughly with soap and hot water.

10. Disinfect tools, instruments, hard surfaces, and clothing used during the disposal.[*]

Gremlin eventually stopped coming around. My neighbors, including James from next door, asked what had happened to him. Months later, James confessed that, like Tweety, Gremlin had crossed paths with his dog Rocky.

"I went in the backyard and saw something white covered in red stains lying on the ground," James told me. "I said, 'Uh oh. I think Rocky got Jodi's cat.'"

My neighbors had pretended to not know what happened because they thought I'd get upset that their dog had killed Gremlin. That I'd be inconsolable about his death. But I knew survival of the fittest even applied to animals in the hood. I always said Gremlin moved too damn slow and was too daring. Cats kill birds. Super gangsta cats steal food from less gangsta cats. And unleashed dogs mangle unsuspecting, slow-moving cats in their backyard. Still, I missed the little guy. I hoped his death was a quick one.

I now have a white French bulldog named Buster, whose big, brown eyes, mushed-in face, and food-stealing, irreverent ways remind me of Gremlin. I keep Buster on a tight leash when we go on walks. He's

---

* "Reporting Dead Wildlife," New York State Department of Environmental Conservation. Accessed May 21, 2023. https://www.dec.ny.gov/animals/6957.html. "Dead Bird Reporting," Louisiana Office of Public Health, Infectious Disease Epidemiology Section. Accessed May 21, 2023. https://ldh.la.gov/assets/oph/Center-PHCH/Center-CH/infectious-epi/WNV/DeadBird/Deadbirds.pdf.

slow-moving and so chunky that a passerby once asked if Buster was a baby pig. He'd be a juicy meal.

A neighbor's unleashed pit bull once stuck his big head through the front door of my building as I held it open for me and Buster to enter. I closed the door on the pit bull's head as an unsuspecting Buster sniffed for food in a corner. That's when the pit bull's owner thought it wise to finally come leash him and lead him away.

Me and Buster steer clear of big dogs and backyards.

Granny's front porch had always been a haven for souls in need. When I was little, before we got bars installed around the porch's perimeter, homeless people would sleep there overnight. Granny brought them food in the morning before they took off on stolen children's bicycles or by foot.

Granny also fed the neighborhood birds. She used to keep a glass jar full of food scraps on the kitchen counter between the stove and sink. The jar, which had originally held duck sauce, contained leftovers from each meal. Grits after they turned cold and hard, and their bottom congealed into a silky smooth, slimy slate. Unfinished strawberry Pop-Tarts. Beets I stuffed into the jar when Granny wasn't looking. All the food combined into an unappealing mush that released an equally unappealing smell whenever we removed the top. Each night after dinner, we would empty the bones from our plates into the garbage can and scrape the remainder of our plates' contents into the jar on the counter.

After Granny washed the dishes, she'd take the trash and food jar outside. She would sweep up paper, cigarettes, beer cans, discarded takeout containers, leaves, and other debris from the sidewalk and gutter in front of our house. She'd then empty the jar's contents onto the sidewalk, near the curb. Sometimes she'd sing a gospel tune or call out to announce her presence. Dozens of pigeons and other birds would descend around her to partake of their nightly feast. The food would be gone by morning. Our neighbors never complained or swept the food up. They never let their dogs eat the food during their walks. They knew that food was for Granny's birds.

I don't remember when Granny stopped feeding the birds, but she fed them for so long that a dark circle formed on the sidewalk where the leftover food once lay. That shadow lingered for years, like spilled oil.

III.

Die the death of a jaybird. Granny often used this phrase—but she didn't use it to mean have your community gather around you in mourning. She used it to describe how someone might react to an embarrassing situation or shocking news. When you die the death of a jaybird in these situations, you experience an intense emotional reaction that goes beyond mere surprise or embarrassment. It's wishing Calgon or Jesus or aliens would come rescue you and take you away to glory, or anywhere else for that matter. It's that heart-stopping disbelief that leaves your jaw on the floor and your vocal cords paralyzed while you solve math equations in your head to make sense of what is happening to you.

Because I love old Black women and the things old Black women say, *Die the death of a jaybird* is a phrase I've adopted. Like the time I went to lunch with this cute guy and dug into my purse for my phone so we could exchange numbers before returning to work. I died the death of a jaybird when I pulled out an Always brand sanitary napkin in its peach plastic wrapping instead of my phone. *He's a medical student so he'll understand,* I thought. He never called me.

Sometimes my inner petty takes over and I intentionally try to induce jaybird-like death in people who deserve it. Like the time my white colleague told me that his wife, who was also white, would never vote for Barack Obama or any other Black person.

"Why not?" I asked him.

"Because she had two Black women bosses who fired her and were mean," he replied as he laughed.

Here's a public service announcement for people with racist loved ones: 1) Black people do not think your family member's racism is funny—not even the Black people with whom you are friendly; and 2) Keep those stories to yourself, especially if you didn't say or do anything to correct or educate your racist loved one.

My colleague's lack of prudence in sharing his wife's disdain for Black people activated my petty superpowers.

"Your wife is a racist and so are you for lying next to her every night," I replied.

Upon hearing my comment, he immediately died the death of a jaybird.

His face turned red with anger, and he waved his arms around while yelling, "How could you say such a thing?"

He stopped speaking to me for a month, and then apologized for sharing that story and for his reaction to my comment.

Other times I merely fantasize about making other people die the death of a jaybird. On my way to work one day, I thought about a meeting I wasn't looking forward to. *I should get a doctor's note that says I can't see certain people more than once a month because they cause me gastrointestinal upset*, I thought. My boss would die the death of a jaybird if I ever submitted such a note.

Then, for the first time in my life, I wondered about the phrase's origins. *How do jaybirds die? How did Granny become an expert on the manner of their deaths?* I'd never heard anyone else use the phrase—not even Granny's twin brother or other elderly family members in Florida, where Granny was born and had spent the first twenty-three years of her life.

When I was a boy I used to hear the following about the jaybird. Most birds in our climate become quiet in the middle
of the day, and this is said to be a characteristic of the jaybird
in the South. The Negroes have the saying that the jaybird
is quiet because during the middle of the day he goes to hell
to carry brimstone for the use of the devil. And when a Negro would catch a jaybird, he would wring its head off and
say, "You won't carry down no sulphur to hell to burn up dis
nigger."

REVEREND GEORGE W. LAY, EASTERN N.C.[*]

Enslaved and freed African Americans in the South feared the jaybird and believed it was Satan's friend and messenger. The jaybird "is
a very beautiful bird, but its beauty is only feather deep. The negro
of the field and quarters looks upon it with pious horror, and always
hums some sort of hymn when it is around."[†]

According to some accounts, the jaybird visited hell on Fridays
to gossip with Satan and returned to earth on Sundays. Others indi-
cate that the jaybird visited hell on Sundays. Depending on the re-
gion and source, it is said that the jaybird visited the underworld once
a year, every week, or every day. In addition to believing the jaybird
carried news of earthly goings-on to Satan, Black folks believed the
jaybird carried either a stick or a varying number of grains of sand to

---

[*] Newman Ivey White and Wayland D. Hand (eds.), *The Frank C. Brown Collection of North Carolina Folklore: Vol. VII: Popular Beliefs and Superstitions from North Carolina*, (Durham, NC: Duke University Press, 1964), 395.

[†] Cora Linn Daniels and Charles McClellan Stevens (eds.), *Encyclopaedia of Superstitions, Folklore, and the Occult Sciences of the World: A Comprehensive Library of Human Belief and Practice in the Mysteries of Life, Volume II* (Chicago: J.H. Yewdale & Sons, 1903), 654.

hell to make its flames burn hotter. There were also differing narratives about what Black folks would do when they saw a jaybird. They might ignore it, run away from it, or kill it by throwing stones at it or by some other means.

Among the negroes of the South, the jaybird is regarded with grave distrust. It is the counsellor, guide and friend of "Ol' Marse Sat'n" himself. The amount of confidence established years ago between the devil and the jaybird is to the African mind enormous. Plantation uncles and aunties believe that when Beelzebub can spare time from frying operations he visits the earth, and he and the jaybird hold a conference of the powers, devising ways and means wherein and whereby to ensnare the weak and feeble mind. Before this combination the dreaded voodoo charm sinks into insignificance in its evil-working powers. There is no defense against it save "rasslin'" in prayer. This is highly esteemed, as a more arduous "rasslin'" the less work will be done in the field the next day.

ENCYCLOPAEDIA OF SUPERSTITIONS, FOLKLORE, AND THE OCCULT SCIENCES OF THE WORLD[*]

Granny loved to recite the Bible scripture, "Life and death are in the power of the tongue." She believed that the words we use can change our circumstances and lives. But her belief about the power of the word was about more than positive thinking. For Granny, and

---

[*] Ibid., 653.

the Pentecostal churches in which I was raised, words were an extension of God. When we spoke in tongues, it was God breathing His
words into us and that message coming out as gibberish or an unknown language not taught in any school or contained in any text-
book. A language that only those with the Holy Ghost could speak or
understand. When Granny prophesied or wrote in the spirit in shapes
and symbols that resembled a toddler's doodlings, her acts were a
physical manifestation of God speaking through her to deliver a message to others about events that would happen in the future. Granny
taught me that the power of life and death and all things is in the power
of the tongue and the pen.

The Yoruba also believe in the power of the word. Olodumare
breathes àṣẹ—the spiritual power to create—into everything. Gods
and spirits. Humans and ancestors. Animals and nature. Even the
language contained in conversations, prayers, curses, and songs is
powerful enough to create change. All women are born with the power
to create and the power of the word. Iyami travel to the astral or spiritual plane, from where they wield the power of the word to their will.

Words and birds changed meaning during the Middle Passage, somewhere between West Africa and the Saint Helena Island plantation
on which my enslaved ancestors toiled in South Carolina. In Yoruba
theology, birds were revered messengers and symbolized the spiritual
powers of the Iyami women. In the American South, jaybirds were re-
viled co-conspirators and emissaries of Satan. If a Black person caught
sight of one, they ensured the jaybird's death would be painful, sudden,
quick, unexpected—much like experiencing embarrassment. It now
made sense why Granny, who was born in the South, used the phrase
"die the death of a jaybird" to describe situations in which someone
was or might become painfully embarrassed. But I wondered how

the symbolism of birds and the nature of their actions and words had changed over time and continents. Like African resources and borders and people, so much of African and Black American culture has been pillaged and transformed by colonization and captivity.

Die the death of a jaybird. I may not know how the phrase made its way to the South, but Granny made it her own. Now it belongs to me. I laugh and utter a *chile* or a *gurrlll* before slipping the phrase into conversations about some jaw-dropping event or another. I imagine Granny years earlier sitting with her feet crossed, the telephone to her ear as she throws her head back, laughs, and utters the same phrase to a friend on the other end of her call. She taught me to love birds and believed all God's creatures deserve to be cared for.

Birds, especially jays, make me think of Granny. A keeper of the birds. A healer. A writer and messenger of God. Oftentimes misunderstood. A bird flying high. A bird, finally free.

IV.

The female deity Odu had the power of the bird. The Orisas Ogun, Obatala, Odua, and Obaluaiye had gifted her four small calabashes and each one contained items associated with the power of its Orisa.[*] Odu became elderly and so confused that she packed her most valuable possession, her power, into the four small calabashes. She then placed them into one large calabash.

Granny's Alzheimer's disease was accompanied by the delusion that people were stealing her belongings. She went to great lengths to

---

[*] Olalekan Azeez Oduntan, "Spiritual Consecration: Igba Iwa-Odu (Ose Oyeku)." Accessed March 23, 2023. http://www.olaleone.org/2023/03/spiritual-consecration-igba-iwa-odu-ose.html.

hide her things. She removed her clothes from the closet, put them in plastic bags, and hid them in various places—drawers, behind her recliner chair, in her hamper, in the washing machine. I once found her favorite shoes, brown suede Naturalizer sneakers, in a plastic bag under her pillow.

When Granny's friend, Mother King, stayed with Granny so that I could attend a cousin's wedding in Florida, Granny was so paranoid that she packed up her most valuable possessions into numerous plastic bags and placed them in our red shopping cart. The bags contained all kinds of things one might need when traveling from your bedroom to the kitchen: clothes, wigs, shoes, pictures, books, napkins, a coat. She pushed the cart everywhere she went in the house. When Mother King had to go home briefly, Granny refused to go with her because they couldn't bring her shopping cart. Our neighbors kept an eye on Granny and the house until Mother King returned.

A bird flew into our house several months after Granny passed away, although I am not sure how because all the windows were closed. Searching for a way out, it kept flying into the kitchen window at the back of the house. When it grew tired of banging its beak against the glass, it flew through the rest of the adjoining rooms on the first floor—the dining room, living room, Granny's bedroom.

When it reached Granny's room at the front of the house, it stood on top of the closet at the foot of her bed before settling on her dresser across the room. It flapped its wings and attempted to fly, and then fell off the edge of the dresser onto the floor. I picked the fallen bird up and placed it back on the dresser. I thought it might be Granny reincarnated or that Granny's spirit had sent it. The bird recovered and flew out of her room.

I tried to guide it with a broom towards the open window in the kitchen. Perhaps I opened a back window because I'd unconsciously remembered the belief that you must leave a back window open in order for a dead person's soul to travel through it and be free. Granny's soul needed to rest. She needed to go. To be at peace. To stop banging into things and falling onto the floor. Finally, more exhausted than the bird, I went to Granny's bedroom and closed its French doors so the bird would not reenter. I climbed into Granny's bed and took a nap. When I awoke, the bird was gone.

6

A Laying On of Hands

I.

I began to grieve the loss of Granny long before her death. Since childhood, her death was the thing I feared most. It even haunted me in my dreams. Whenever I had nightmares as a kid, I'd go to Granny's bedroom and pat her arm until she stirred awake.

"Ma, I had a bad dream," I'd tell her.

"Really? Tell me about it," she'd say. I'd then climb into her bed and lie beside her in the dark. Sometimes I lied about having a nightmare just so I could sleep with her. As I recited my dream, she'd interrupt with an occasional question or a "Yes, Lord." In one of the few dreams from my childhood I remember, a white woman sat atop a horse carriage. She appeared to be leaving rather than arriving. Although the dream occurred in black and white, the white woman looked like a character straight out of the TV show "Little House on the Prairie": her hair was pushed up high into a bouffant, and she wore a light-colored, fitted high-collared blouse with ruffles down the front and a dark-colored wide, long skirt that looked like it was made of material that made your skin itch. Although she was white, I sensed that she was still Granny—just in a different body. It was as if Granny's spirit had transferred from her Jheri-curl-wig-wearing body to that of this white woman. For reasons I could not explain, the dream saddened me. It felt as if Granny were leaving me, as if she had transformed into something else—something unfamiliar and unreachable. I tried to convey this sense of loss to Granny when I woke her up and climbed into her bed to tell her about my dream.

"You know how you would feel if someone died?" I asked Granny.
"Yes," she replied.
"Well, that's how I feel about you."

Pastor M's funeral is the first one I remember ever attending. He pastored a small congregation in a storefront church that was always drafty and always smelled and looked like it was under construction. The night of his funeral, I held Granny's hand and looked up at him in his casket. He was a pretty man with curly, slicked down hair. His wide, stiff nostrils seemed to be moving.

"Ma, he's breathing," I told Granny as I hid behind her.

Any dead, embalmed person looks like they're breathing if you stare long enough. I was afraid of dead people for a long time after that.

Prayer and deliverance are rituals. Granny used to always say, "God will use the foolish to confound the wise." No matter how silly or inexplicable they looked, rituals were a symbolic way of demonstrating faith and a vehicle for miracles. In the church I attended as a child, various types of medical equipment lined the walls of the lobby. Canes along with neck, back, and leg braces hung neatly as if they were a museum exhibit. These items formerly belonged to people who'd been healed of their illnesses. I can imagine the scenes of their owners' deliverance, the same scenes that played out during many church services I've attended.

The Anatomy of a Healing

1. The preacher lays hands and blessed oil on the prayer recipient's forehead and/or site of affliction.

2. The preacher prays in English and in tongues, commanding the illness and the evil spirits it rode in on to leave the prayer recipient's body.

3. Members of the audience provide reinforcement by praying, clapping their hands, and speaking in tongues.

4. Audience members sometimes point one hand towards the prayer recipient in communal prayer to God.

5. The prayer recipient catches the Holy Ghost and falls backwards onto the floor. Deacons and ushers wait behind the prayer recipient, ready to catch their fall. If the prayer recipient is a woman, then women ushers place a white cloth over her legs so onlookers won't see all her family jewels.

6. When the prayer recipient emerges from their prayer stupor, they may immediately believe God has healed them of their sickness, as demonstrated by decreased pain or increased flexibility and mobility. They may walk/run/hop around without their assistive devices to prove they have been healed.

7. Sometimes the prayer recipient does not realize they've been healed until several days later or their next doctor's appointment.

8. Once the prayer recipient realizes they've been healed, they release themselves from the shackles of their assistive devices and emerge as new creatures.

Pastors laid hands on us. Granny laid hands on me. But all touch ain't created equal.

"I felt uncomfortable whenever he prayed for me and put his hands on my back," a friend told me several years ago about a pastor we'd known as children. She didn't need to say what she meant by "uncomfortable." I'd felt the same unease the last time I saw him, when he placed his hand on my back and rubbed it as he spoke to me. His touch raised the hair on my skin, echoing all the times men touched me unnecessarily just to cop a feel.

II.

My fear of Granny dying always lurked when each of her many illnesses reared its ugly head. My earliest memory of Granny's ill health was when I was around nine or so. Her stomach was in so much pain one night that she rubbed it as she rolled around on the red shaggy carpet of her bedroom.

"Ohhhhhh Lordie, have mercy on my soul," she kept saying.

I had seen Granny pray for and anoint people with blessed oil many times. She consecrated bottles of Goya extra-virgin olive oil by praying over them and letting them sit on her altar for twenty-one days. Her altar, which she covered with a white lace cloth, was on top of an old floor model television that stopped working when I was a kid after I stuck a penny in it. In addition to the Goya bottles of oil, Granny's altar contained a large open Bible; a mounted pair of brown ceramic hands with their palms open; pictures of family members; and a few rosaries. Although we weren't Catholic, Granny collected rosaries and often recited the Hail Mary prayer. After the twenty-one days were up, Granny then poured the oil into smaller bottles and distributed them to people so that they could anoint themselves. She also kept some for herself. If this oil had the power to heal others, then maybe it could heal Granny.

I grabbed a bottle of blessed oil, poured some into my small hand,

and rubbed it on her bare stomach. I then prayed for her. I imagine that I uttered the same words of prayer Granny frequently used:

> Lord, stretch out Your nail-scarred hands and heal yo chile.
> Ya never lost a battle and I know that ya never will.
> I'll tell dying men and women of Your goodness everywhere.
> These and all the many blessings I ask in Your name.
> Amen.

After I pulled her shirt down, I opened a Bible to the 23rd Psalm and placed it face down on her stomach. *Yea, though I walk through the valley of death, I will fear no evil: for thou art with me . . . thou anointest my head with oil.*

During the school year, Granny usually restricted my TV time. On this night, however, she attempted to distract me.

"If I let you watch TV, do you promise to be a good girl?"

"Yes."

I turned the television on and changed the channel to *Hill Street Blues,* but I couldn't concentrate on the show. Instead, I attempted to bargain with God. It was the first time I offered to give God something in exchange for granting me a miracle. God, I promise to be good if you make my Granny alright, I silently prayed. I would make this deal with God many more times throughout my life. No matter how fervent our prayers and sincere our hearts, we eventually run out of bargaining chips.

On the first Saturday of each month, our church had communion and foot-washing service. These services were a full-body experience during which we ate and drank of Jesus's body and reenacted the ritual of Jesus washing His disciples' feet. The women and girls dressed in all white and wrapped our heads in white scarves. The men wore black suits with white shirts and no ties. During communion, we filed out of our seats row by row, walked to the front of the church, up the ramp to the top, where the pastor and deacons waited to hand us shot glasses of Welch's grape juice and broken pieces of matzo crackers, then we went back down the ramp to our seats.

After communion, we began the foot-washing portion of the service. Ushers passed out hand towels and water-filled basins. We paired up by gender, with the boys and men gathering at the front of the church to wash each other's feet. After the pastor read from John 13 (*If I then, your Lord and Teacher, have washed your feet, you also ought to wash one another's feet*), we leaned down or got on our knees and said a prayer as we washed one another's feet, one foot at a time. I struggled not to laugh as Granny's fingers swept the water around and brushed against my feet. The boys and men were lucky because they could take off their socks, have their feet washed, and then dry their feet completely before putting their socks and shoes back on. The girls and women, on the other hand, had to dip our stockinged feet into the water. No matter how much we rubbed the towels over our feet, some amount of dampness remained. Foot washing was an act of service and humility, each person nurturing the other.

A man who went to our church was the first person I knew who died of AIDS. He was very tall and bald. When I was a little girl, he used to bend down and let me rub his head. By the time he was dying, he'd become a pariah and folks from our church wouldn't visit him—not even to pray for him or give him communion. They thought they'd catch his illness by touching him or breathing the same air. Granny sometimes went to his house and cared for him. The night of his funeral, I kept looking over at his children. I wondered what it must feel like to lose a parent and how they could be so calm.

I knew a lot of people who died from AIDS. Friends. Church members. Single. Married, with one spouse infecting the other. Intravenous drug users. Drug-free. Straight. Gay. Bisexual. Out. Closeted or "on the down low." I knew so many people who'd died from AIDS that I was more afraid of getting HIV than I was of getting pregnant. At least I could get an abortion. HIV and AIDS were commonly viewed as a death sentence.

I knew so many people who'd died of AIDS that I wanted to become a healer and find a cure for the disease. I wanted to be an infectious disease specialist before I could even properly pronounce or spell the word *infectious*. In high school, I spent a summer working on the AIDS hospice unit of a local nursing home. I also subscribed to the print version of *The New York Times*. I scoured the "Science Times" section every Tuesday for articles about AIDS and other infectious diseases and collected my favorite ones in a folder. Despite my medical aspirations, my college science classes and my fear of blood and gore got the best of me.

There's a YouTube video of a popular Black pastor praying for people at church during the altar call. Several people are standing with their hands raised as they pray or wait for the pastor to lay hands on them; others are stretched out on the floor, silently or speaking in tongues, because the pastor has already prayed for them. The pastor walks over to a Black woman who has her hands raised and lays hands on her. His hand covers the top half of her face, from her forehead down to her nose. The pastor pushes the woman's head back a couple of times and she remains standing. He then pokes her chest with his index finger while saying "Why you come up here for me to pray for you and lock yo knees? Go sit down if you don't want me to pray for ya." He continues fussing at her, saying "What you come here for? You don't come to receive, don't come. Cus I ain't makin ya get nuthin." Offended by her preemptive measures to avoid falling backwards, he walks away without praying for her or others standing nearby.

This woman is both a superhero and the embodiment of my altar call fears. Going to the altar to get prayer is one big trust exercise. Unfortunately, I don't trust others to catch me and I don't trust my bones to hold up. Whenever preachers laid hands on me, I struggled against the force of their hands as the blessed oil dripped down my face, temporarily blinding me. Sometimes I might allow the preacher to push my head back. I feared giving way, giving in, and falling backwards. When I fall, I sprain and break things. I once fell while running down the steps to pick up a Grubhub order. That hamburger and fries cost me a torn ligament and a broken ankle that had to be reconstructed with a metal plate and screws. Maybe the woman at the altar also feared falling. Maybe she, like myself, has never caught the Holy Ghost or "shouted." Like me, maybe she didn't feel the need to perform her faith or pretend that she felt something she didn't.

The pastor's ego was bruised because the woman at the altar revealed his lack of power—or the absence of God's power working through him. When he laid hands on people, they fell out under the power of his hands and gravity, not the Holy Ghost. He was angry because she exercised her agency and refused to play along. Why must the Holy Ghost be so aggressive and intrusive? It should be able to work miracles without the pastor breaking a person's neck and smothering their face with his hands. Surely, the Holy Ghost can reach people while they are standing up. The woman at the altar, this superhero, said *Not today, Satan!* Dear Queen, I and the rest of the Locked Knees Delegation salute you.

III.

I started to grieve the loss of Granny when she was diagnosed with Alzheimer's disease. I became frightfully aware that we would never return to our old lives and that there would come a time when she wouldn't know my name—or hers. Periodically, I would ask her questions to make sure she still remembered life's most important facts.

> What's your name, Granny?
>> *Annie Lee McKinney.*
> When's your birthday?
>> *April 23, 1937.*
> What's my name?
>> *Jodi Savage.*
> Who's the president?
>> *Barack Obama . . .*
>>> *Marack Barama . . .*
>>>> *The Black man . . .*
>>>>> *I don't know.*

I often asked myself, *Will today be the day?* The day Granny can no longer return to the present. I lived in constant fear of what was to come and worked hard to hold on to the past and the present.

———

Granny's hallucinations landed her in the geriatric psychiatric ward twice. She was a social butterfly during her first hospital stay, when she served as the self-appointed spiritual adviser to her fellow patients. She'd also notify them whenever they had a call on the phone outside her room. During Granny's second stay a few years later, however, she was much more reserved and anxious. She had good reason to be. "A man was in here," Granny told me when I arrived at her room on discharge day to pack her belongings. I thought the "man" was another one of her hallucinations, until I saw a man on the unit wearing Granny's pink and red pajama pants with the teddy bears on them. I also spotted Granny's teddy bear on a couch in the family room. I'd never liked the idea of co-ed units, and Granny's room was always at the end of the hall, furthest away from the eyes and protection of the nurses and other staff.

"Do you want them back?" a nurse asked when I complained about Granny's stolen pants.

"Nah, he can keep them."

Clothes—and supervision—were often in short supply on that unit. On several occasions, I spotted another male patient walking up and down the hall with his hospital gown open in the back and his bare butt cheeks greeting everyone.

It was a wild place. No wonder Granny wanted to get out of there.

When I'd arrived on the unit earlier, I found Granny standing at the nurse's station.

"She's been standing here all morning because she was afraid you wouldn't be able to find her," the nurse told me. "I told her you'd come to her room, but she said she'd rather wait here."

Granny took my hand and squeezed it until it hurt. I didn't want to cause a scene in front of the nurses because we both knew what might happen afterwards. With her lips squeezed as tightly together as our hands, her look was fearful and defiant. "Let go. It's okay. I'm not going to leave you here," I told her as I used my free hand to force our hands apart so that I could complete the check-out paperwork.

IV.

When death began circling Granny, I didn't even recognize it. Up until the night before her final hospitalization, she'd been able to feed herself and was lucid. However, her condition drastically declined by the second day of her hospitalization. She could no longer feed herself, mumbled her words, and began experiencing a new kind of hallucination. As I fed her applesauce, she began talking to family members who had passed away years earlier.

"Ma'Dear, get down from there! You gon' fall and hurt yo self," she said to her mother as she looked up at the wall facing her bed.

"Uh uh. Lilla, don't do that," she admonished her younger sister while looking at a spot beside her invisible mother.

Although hallucinations were normal for her, she had never hallucinated about deceased loved ones. At the time, I didn't know that when people are near death, they sometimes see loved ones who've passed on. Many believe that when a person is near death, family members or friends come to guide them to the next life. I used to think that was some new-age, hocus pocus psychobabble.

I imagined Granny dying peacefully in her sleep without any fanfare. Auntie Annie Lou, who was Granny's maternal aunt and had Alzheimer's years before her, sat on her bedroom floor with her back against her bed one night, took her wig off, and placed it in her lap. My aunt and cousin found her lifeless body like that the next morning. Auntie Annie Lou's actions were deliberate, as if she knew she was going to die that night. Perhaps departed loved ones also came to guide her home and she removed her wig so she could travel light. She died a sudden, peaceful death. I had hoped Granny would have a similar one. But the process of dying can be brutal, protracted, and frightening. It can be hard on a body and soul. It's comforting to know our loved ones may accompany us on our final journeys. When it's my time to go, I hope Granny comes to escort me. I have already decided that if anyone else shows up for me, I will fight them and run away from that light at the end of the tunnel.

I kept track of how far away death was from Granny by keeping tabs on the old man whose room was across the hall from hers. He looked much older and frailer than Granny, his chest heaving up and down from the oxygen being pumped into him. As long as the winds of death passed over him, Granny would be safe—I hoped. And then one day I noticed his room was empty. My heart jumped.

"Where did the old man go?" I asked a nurse while pointing to his room.

"He was moved to a regular room," she replied.

The fact that he had been moved from the Intensive Care Unit to a regular medical unit meant he had greatly improved. If there was hope for him, then Granny still had a chance. And then the woman in the next room, who looked to be in her twenties, passed away. As her family hollered and sobbed, I stood still and looked at Granny hooked up to her own respirator and maze of IV tubes. None of us were safe.

V.

Acceptance of death has two sub-stages: hysteria and a calm resolve. The order varies; the cycle repeats. At some point, I finally accepted the inevitable. It wasn't pretty. During the last week of Granny's life, I slept in her hospital room most nights, cooped up on two recliner chairs pushed together to form a makeshift bed. On one of these nights, I got up and went to the bathroom. I sat on the floor and cried—ugly, loud, desperate sobs. "God, I don't want her to suffer," I muttered through snot and tears. Hysteria. The last morning of Granny's life, a coworker asked me how Granny was doing and whether there was anything she could do for me. "Pray that her suffering ends," I replied. Calm resolve. Granny passed away a couple of hours later.

Once calm resolve sets in, acceptance imposes an air of finality. It makes way for a definite course of action. Whenever I finally accept something, become convinced that a certain outcome is inevitable, I become a decisive taskmaster. I determine the things that need doing, and I get busy doing them. There is comfort in busyness. Busyness is another way to grieve. I began planning Granny's homegoing service before she took her last breath. This was the last gift I would be able to give her. I bought a small, red spiral-bound notebook and designated it as Granny's funeral notebook. I wrote notes about my conversations with the funeral director. I also made a list of things I'd need for her homegoing, including her favorite songs and Bible scriptures.

I also thought about the funeral tribute I wanted to write for her. Granny taught me how to write about the dead. Whenever a friend, church member, or family member passed away, she would write a tribute to them. The tribute's header contained the person's name, date of birth, and date of death. Granny wrote it in the form of a flight announcement, as if the person were flying off to heaven.

ANNIE LEE MCKINNEY

FLIGHT 100

ARRIVAL: APRIL 23, 1937

DEPARTURE: JUNE 27, 2011

Fancier than an obituary, the body of these one-pagers highlighted special aspects of the deceased person's life and personality. Granny loved finding the right words to capture someone's life. Her tributes were a team effort: She would write them out in longhand and I'd type them up and print out copies. She would then read the tributes at the honoree's homegoing and pass them out to the attendees. The looks of appreciation on loved ones' faces while listening to Granny's tributes showed me that words can be a salve for grieving hearts.

I wanted to honor Granny with a funeral tribute just as she had done for others, but my words didn't seem sufficient to describe who she was—a woman who loved words, Jesus, and encouraging others. Instead of writing one of Granny's traditional tributes, I decided that her tribute would consist of a list of my favorite sayings of hers—"Grannyisms."

In the wee hours of the morning, when Granny was asleep and the hospital halls were quiet, I curled up in the recliner chair in the corner of Granny's room and began to write.

After a while, I got up and held her hand. I talked to her as nurses and other hospital personnel came in and out of her room to check her temperature and other vitals and draw her blood.

"Granny, remember how you always tell me, 'Don't kiss me. You gon' mess up my pretty skin.'" I laughed as I wiped imaginary germs off my cheek, imitating Granny.

"Or how you always tell me, 'Never esteem anyone higher than yourself.'"

Granny looked at me intently with bright smiling eyes. She was so alert. Her eyes were sharp—she saw me, saw into me. She looked as if she were willing her eyes to say what her mouth could not. I had seen that look before. A few nights before she went into the hospital, we were watching TV in her bedroom. I was sitting on the ottoman and she sat in the chair across from me. When I looked over at her, she was staring and smiling at me. I smiled back at her. We didn't need to say a word. Her eyes said how much she loved me.

At Granny's hospital bedside, my left hand in hers, I recited one of her favorite Bible scriptures. "I will look to the hills from whence cometh my help, for my help cometh from the Lord!" I imitated Granny's pious voice and demeanor, shaking my head and flailing my right hand. Then she squeezed my hand tightly, letting me know she understood—or perhaps letting me know that she also knew our time together was limited. That was the last time I was able to hold Granny's hands while she was alive. The last time she was able to understand me. The last time she really saw me.

As my brother and I waited in our mother's hospice room for someone from the funeral home to come pick up her body, I looked at her
hands and realized that she and Granny had the same hands. I'd
never noticed this before, perhaps because I hadn't spent enough
time around her. Her hands had not touched me as often as Granny's
had. Although my mother's hands were smaller than Granny's, they
both had long, bony fingers, fingernails short to the meat, a maze of
veins that populated their tops. My mother's hands, a telltale sign of
her sixty-one years, were incongruous with her youthful face.

My mother's hands remained free and I was able to hold them until the end. Granny's hands were swallowed up in the doctors' efforts
to save her. Nurses placed inflated mittens on Granny's hands to prevent her from pulling at the tubes coming out of her veins and mouth.
Eventually, she was too sedated to fight any longer, but the slightest
touch pained her. I could no longer hold her hands to comfort her or
show her that I loved her. I would no longer feel her hands on my forehead as she prayed for me or rubbed it with blessed oil. Never again
would I hear her claps as she prayed and sang. I would not hold her
hands again until after she left me.

Because of breast cancer, I've grown used to doctors poking, rubbing,
pressing, lifting, and pushing my breasts. When I went in for a chest
X-ray, I immediately started taking off my blouse and bra. "You don't
need to do that," the X-ray tech said with a "Damn, you just get un-
dressed for er'body, huh?" look on her face. By the time I lay on a table
as strangers prepped me for radiation, it no longer mattered that one
of the radiation techs was a man. He lifted the sheet underneath me to
adjust my position on the table. The techs moved my upper torso and
breasts into awkward positions to make sure the small green dots tat-

tooed on my skin lined up with the radiation field. I lay there with no resistance, no effort to move one way or another, no thought of shrinking or hiding.

I am touched so frequently that I compare the nature of doctors' touches. One doctor touched my breasts hesitantly, like the people who hold on to your fingertips instead of fully shaking your hand. Another pressed my breasts so lightly that I worried she might not feel my tumor. One doctor really got up in there. Her presses and probes were so hard I thought my breasts would turn inside out and stay that way. It's all necessary and I usually feel like a science experiment when it's over.

I visited my new primary care physician because I'd had heart palpitations for several months. She was the first Black doctor I'd had in years. She began with a breast exam by firmly pressing my breasts in concentric circles. Afterwards, I sat up on the table and she examined my ears and mouth. She bent down with a soft rubber hammer and hit each of my knees with it to test my reflexes. Then I suddenly felt something happening at my feet. Rather than asking me to remove my shoes, the doctor had taken them off for me. She held her hand under each foot and told me to push down, then held her hand on top and told me to push up. I was thankful I'd recently gotten a pedicure and worn my cute shoes. We discussed my medical history and she informed me that I was considered morbidly obese because of my height, weight, and body mass index. I knew I was fat, but *damn*. "Morbidly obese" has a whole different ring (and set of health risks) to it. We discussed lifestyle changes I should make, as well as plans for follow-up care and a referral to a cardiologist.

The doctor looked at my arms and hands.

"Is it usually difficult to get blood?" she asked.

"Yup." Having my blood drawn is always a drag because my veins are hard to find. I once joked to a nurse that my veins have rhythm and twerk because they moved each time she inserted the needle.

"Did you see the Elizabeth Holmes Netflix series?" I asked.

"No, but I did see the documentary."

"I really wish she'd been able to make her blood test contraption work so I wouldn't have to keep getting my blood drawn."

She laughed and instructed a tech to give me two cups of water to drink before attempting to draw my blood. The doctor then walked me to the lab. Before I knew it, she was hugging me. That visit left me near tears.

When she took my shoes off and when she embraced me, it dawned on me: I'd been missing a laying on of hands.

It feels as if I am always in a doctor's office for one thing or another. There is always something that needs to be monitored, administered, checked out, tested, or taken. Medical care is often impersonal, perfunctory, rushed. I go from one cold exam room to another. Sometimes I lose track of where I need to be and when I need to be there. In all my rushing from one place to another, I sometimes forget to feel. But my doctor remembered to feel. There was no judgment, disgust, or discomfort in her movements. Just honesty and compassion and another Black woman who *saw* me.

When she bent down in her heels and black dress to remove my shoes, her actions reminded me of the sacred foot-washing services I attended as a child. I was transported back in time, when Granny knelt and cupped my feet in her hands as she prayed and sprinkled them with water. Her posture of supplication an entreaty to God, her hands an instrument to cleanse, to anoint, to serve. Like Granny, my doctor reminded me that my body was holy and worthy of care.

7

I'm Too Pretty to Die Tonight

Wednesday, October 14, 2020

My mother, Cheryl, whom I hadn't seen in almost a year, sent me a text message to find out if I had scheduled my mammogram.

Wed, Oct 14, 3:53 PM
Hey Jodi what's going on have you been to the doctor yet I hope you're not procrastinating about this situation please don't be like me put it off put it off and then when you decide to do something it's almost too late I love you please call me later

My mother knew my fears all too well. She had stage 4 breast cancer that had spread to her lungs, liver, and bones. Five years earlier, she told me that her breast had been swollen and sore for months, and that it hurt to lift her arm or sleep on her left side.

"Why did you wait so long to go to the doctor?" I asked her.

"I was scared," she replied.

She finally made an appointment when the pain became unbearable. By that time, there were numerous tumors in her breast, and she was diagnosed with stage 3 breast cancer. She had a mastectomy of her left breast and had nineteen lymph nodes removed.

Wednesday, October 7, 2020

The day before my 42nd birthday was one of extremes. Good and bad. Night and day. That afternoon, I spoke with a literary agent I'd recently queried who was interested in representing me. After our call, I jumped up and down in my living room, attempted to twerk, and did the running man. "I think she's the one," I yelled to my French bulldog, Buster, while he silently looked up at me with big, round eyes that seemed to question whether he should bark for help.

That evening, I played with Buster by rubbing his face and head and then quickly snatching my hand away so that he would jump up. In the midst of our game, I pulled my hand back from him too forcefully and wound up hitting my left breast. A sharp pain immediately settled in. When I rubbed the spot I'd hit, the pain did not subside. I didn't think I had hit myself hard enough to cause so much soreness. I massaged my breast more deeply, firmly pressing down into my flesh in circular motions to get relief. That's when I felt it—a small, hard ball about a half inch from my nipple. It felt like a marble wedged deep into my tissue. A speck of peach-colored skin sat atop the lump, as if it were the origin point of vitiligo that would eventually spread to the rest of my brown-skinned body.

I called my friend Janine in a panic. When she didn't answer, I sent her a text.

Wed, Oct 7, 9:34 PM
I think I have breast cancer. Where you at? I got a lumpy boob.

Thursday, October 8, 2020

On my birthday, I woke up to a text from my mother.

> *Thu, Oct 8, 7:20 AM*
> Happy birthday to you happy birthday to you . . . thinking about you call me later I'm getting ready to go to my group program

My mother was in a drug rehab program in Miami for her crack cocaine addiction and attended various individual and group therapy sessions throughout the day. I was happy to see her text because it was one of the few times she'd ever contacted me on my birthday—she was usually in jail or out getting high.

I tried not to think about the lump I'd found the previous night. My birthday celebration options were limited because we were in the middle of the COVID-19 pandemic. We couldn't go out for dinner, catch a Broadway show, or even get our nails done. I still took the day off work. Janine and I went to Greenlight Bookstore, where I bought *Luster* by Raven Leilani, *On Earth We're Briefly Gorgeous* by Ocean Vuong, and *I Love Myself When I Am Laughing . . .* a Zora Neale Hurston reader edited by Alice Walker. Afterwards, Janine treated me to a chocolate cupcake and iced hot chocolate.

"Gurl, what if my lump is cancer?" I said as we walked home.

"You do not have cancer," Janine replied. "It's probably nothing, but you should get it checked out anyway." Still unconvinced, I tried to swallow my anxiety as I sipped my iced hot chocolate.

Saturday, October 17, 2020

Although my mother lived in Florida and we spent more time estranged than not, she was one of the first people I told about my
lump. She was the only person I knew who'd understand what I was
going through. The only person who could mother me. And mothering me is what she did, in the best way she knew how.

> *Sat, Oct 17, 10:20 AM*
> Jody I'm good I'm praying for you and with you and I want you to
> know you don't have to do this by yourself like I did I love you Jody
> call me later love you and God got you the same way he has me

The correct spelling of my first name is J-O-D-I. Although my
mother's spelling of my name alternated between Jodi with an "i" and
Jody with a "y," she usually spelled it with a "y." It baffled me that she
consistently misspelled the name she had given me, but I was used to
it and never bothered to correct her. It was another reminder that she
had not raised me and only occasionally needed to write my name. Her
misspellings and run-on sentences reflected her fidgety nature and inability to slow down and focus. Bipolar disorder and decades of crack
cocaine use caused her mind and body to continuously race from one
place to another. She'd been that way for so long that I didn't know
if nature or nurture had made her like that. It was hard to say which
came first: her addiction, her mental illness, or her racing thoughts.

Friday, October 23, 2020

I laid on the table as the tech rubbed gel onto my breasts and under-
arms. The image of my left breast on the black screen lit up in red,

purple, blue, and yellow as the tech rubbed the wand over different sections of my slippery skin. The image was most colorful in the area where I'd felt the lump—the lump that hadn't even appeared on the mammogram I'd taken earlier that day, thanks to my dense breasts. I looked up at the screen and tried to interpret what the pictures and colors meant, but my efforts were useless.

"I'll be right back. I'm gonna either come back with the doctor or with some instructions from her," the tech told me. She seemed more serious, worried.

Why did she need to go speak with the doctor? Why would the doctor need to see me now? I wondered. This couldn't be good news. My eyes became watery, and a single tear fell down my face. I willed myself to not freak out and quickly wiped it dry so the stern, robotic tech would not have the awkward job of comforting me. I worried that if I started crying, she would look at me like I was unhinged, unsure of what to say or do. Then we'd both be uncomfortable. I didn't need that on top of the fear I was already feeling about my results.

When the tech returned with the radiologist, the doctor introduced herself and reviewed the ultrasound images of my left breast on the screen.

"You have to return first thing Monday morning for a biopsy," the doctor told me. "Although we can see a mass, we don't know what it is. And one of your lymph nodes is abnormally shaped."

She asked whether I had contact information for a breast surgeon.

"Yes. My gynecologist referred me to one and I have an appointment the week after next."

"Who did your GYN refer you to?" she asked. I gave her the name of the surgeon.

"Okay, she's the best. I was going to give you her name if you had said someone else," the doctor replied. "See if you can get an earlier appointment."

It became harder for me to breathe.

Saturday, October 24, 2020

During my nap, I dreamt that I was trying to figure out who would take care of Granny if I died. I considered sending her to go live with her twin brother in Florida. But then I thought about how unhappy she would be in a place she hadn't lived in for almost 60 years. I thought about my job's life insurance policy and any other money I'd be able to leave for her care. In the dream, I wished I had saved more money for her in case something happened to me. I considered telling my friend Nicola about all my insurance information for Granny. I also wondered who would take Granny to her doctor's appointments and check on her. I thought about Janine at first, but my other friend Marilyn was the better choice. She loved helping little old ladies, worked in the medical field, and was older and more grounded.

When I awoke, I remembered that Granny had been dead for nearly ten years. If I did have breast cancer and die, I was relieved that I wouldn't leave anyone behind who needed me. There was no one, other than my dog, depending on me to care for them.

Friday, October 30, 2020

A radiologist called me at about ten o'clock that morning. She explained that the doctor who'd performed my biopsy was out that day, so she was calling on her behalf.

"Unfortunately, the biopsy showed that you have a form of breast cancer called invasive ductal carcinoma. However, the biopsy of your lymph node was negative," the doctor told me.

Invasive ductal carcinoma. It sounded like a foreign language. Cancer is the only word I understood. The doctor explained my diagnosis to me.

"Ductal, meaning it originated in the milk duct, and invasive, meaning it has spread into or invaded the surrounding breast tissue."

"What stage is it?" I asked.

"Your breast surgeon will discuss staging, surgery, and treatment plans with you," she explained. "I'm sorry to have to give you this news on a Friday. I struggled with whether to call you today or wait until Monday."

I put on a fake cheery voice. "Well thank you for calling me today. I would've been anxious all weekend."

After our call ended, I laid on my bed and sobbed.

Mon, Nov 16, 1:18 PM
Hi Jody how are you I had my procedure done this morning to take the fluid [off my lungs] . . . I'm feeling better I'm coming home from hospital today love you

Cheryl often provided me with updates about her health in short, random text messages. I'd then call my brother or another family member for the backstory. My brother explained that the cancer had spread to Cheryl's lungs, causing fluid to accumulate around them. She'd been hospitalized so that doctors could drain the fluid. As my mother lay in a hospital bed recovering from surgery and contending with an increasing number of complications, I was still reeling from my own breast cancer diagnosis, preparing for surgery, and afraid of what my own future held.

Tuesday, November 24, 2020

Two days before Thanksgiving, my friends Jennifer and Joella drove me to a Manhattan outpatient cancer center to have my breast surgery. My surgeon was going to perform a lumpectomy—she was going to remove the tumor in my left breast and several lymph nodes under my arm. Cheryl called me that morning while we were in the car on our way to the city. I put her on speakerphone.

"Hey chile, I'm on my way to surgery," I told her.

"I have an appointment with my oncologist today. What kind of cancer do you have? So I can tell my doctor," Cheryl said. We'd previously discussed needing to compare our breast cancers so that I'd have more information about breast cancer in our family for my genetic counseling.

"I have invasive ductal carcinoma that's estrogen and progesterone positive," I replied.

"You have what?" she asked.

"Invasive ductal carcinoma. That means the cancer started in my milk duct," I explained.

"The milk duct?" she asked.

"What doesn't she understand? The milk or the duct?" Jennifer asked as Joella and I laughed.

"You don't know what a milk duct is? Didn't you give birth to two whole kids?" I asked Cheryl. She laughed.

She later told me that she had infiltrating ductal carcinoma that was estrogen receptor-positive. I learned that "invasive" and "infiltrating" are used interchangeably and that we had the same type of breast cancer. I'd spent my life trying to be my mother's opposite in every way—not wanting to repeat her mistakes or live her life of addiction. I'd prided myself on being responsible and "doing life right." Although genetic testing revealed that I had not inherited the BRCA1 or BRCA2 gene mutation that makes women more likely to develop breast cancer, I was still my mother's child down to the malignant, molecular level.

"Lemme send you some pictures of me," she said.

In the pictures, she looked like she was headed to the club or a night out with the girls instead of an oncology appointment. Her short, salt-and-pepper hair was slicked back, and her midnight blue glasses were perched on her head. She wore blue skinny jeans and a black crop top that stopped just beneath her breast. The accent piece of her outfit was the orange blouse she wore over her crop top—a sheer, puffy number made of tulle. It had a deep cut in the front, revealing her black top underneath, and a thick sash around her waist that flared out into ruffles. Her eyelashes, eyeshadow, and lipstick were perfectly applied, she wore stud earrings, and two necklaces. She did not dress like your average sixty-year-old.

"Go head, sexy momma!" I told her. "Who you lookin' sexy for?"

"I gotta look sexy for my oncologist," she replied.

Her outfits were starkly different from my cancer treatment uniform. The plaid button-down shirts I wore for my medical appointments were easy to get out of when doctors needed to examine my breasts or I needed to undergo imaging tests. A few months later, while I was undergoing radiation treatments, my friend Janine saw me in my daily uniform of plaid shirt, leggings, and pink loafers. "You gotta start dressing better or they're gonna think you're homeless and give you bad medical treatment," she said. I didn't look completely homeless. I applied lotion so I wouldn't be ashy, aluminum-free deodorant so I wouldn't be funky, and combed my hair. I was cute from the neck up.

Friday, February 12, 2021

"Call Justin," Cheryl told me. She was in hospice and wanted me to call my father on three-way.

"Okay. Hold on."

"Hey, Justin Savage," I said when he answered the phone.

"Hey, Jodi Savage! How ya doin'?" This is how we greet one another—by our first and last names. For starters, "Savage" is a cool name. This is also our way of bypassing the awkwardness of me not calling him Dad or Daddy or figuring out what else to call him.

"I'm doin' alright. Cheryl is in hospice and wants to talk to ya. She's on the other line. Hold on."

"Okaaaaay," he said in a what-the-hell-is-going-on way.

"Cheryl, you there?"

"Yup."

"Justin, you on?"

"Uh huh."

"Hey, Cheryl, how ya doin'?" my father asked. Once all three of us were connected, we engaged in the awkward, halting small talk of groups of people who do not normally speak to one another. This conversation was our attempt at normalcy—as if my parents had raised me together as a happily married couple. As if my mother was not in hospice. Still, I laughed and smiled a wide goofy smile as I sat on my bed talking to them.

"What happened to you?" Cheryl asked my father. "I called and you ain't neva pick up the phone."

"Oh, I gotta tell you bout that. We'll talk about that later," he responded, clearly not wanting me to know what was going on. My mother had told me she was going to start hanging out with my father. Perhaps they'd planned to meet, and he'd stood her up.

"You get disability? I need some money," my mother told him.

"No. I'm a stripper. I make too much money to get disability." He said it so smoothly that I almost believed him.

"Nigga, I'm yo wife," she told him.

"I know, but ya left me Cheryl," he responded. Although still legally married, they hadn't been together since I was a baby.

"God told me to tell you to put them Heinekens down," Cheryl said. We did not need divine intervention to know my father should cut down on his alcohol consumption. I guess Cheryl thought he might actually do it if he thought God had delivered a special message just for him.

"I stopped drinking a long time ago," he responded. I had my doubts but kept quiet. Who was I to bust up our happy family time?

"You did?" Cheryl asked.

"Yeah."

"Justin, you want some pocketbook?" she asked him. This is where the conversation went left. "Pocketbook" was a euphemism for vagina, which she'd used to make money during her days as a prostitute. She took great pride in her pocketbook. She once told me, "I ain't finna use up my pocketbook. My Gucci, my Chanel, my Louis Vuitton. I got name-brand pocketbook."

I was afraid of how my father would respond to my mother's pocketbook offering.

"But you gotta pay for it, tho. I don't give out nothing for free," she told my father.

"Cheryl, you know we don't do that no mo. Don't talk that way," Justin said. "Jodi, I ain't mean for you to hear all that," he added.

"I ain't mean to hear all that either," I responded. I was embarrassed enough for the three of us.

"We gotta get married again," my mother told him.

"Cheryl, we still married."

"Oh."

Before we got off the phone, Justin made plans to visit her in hospice.

"Call before you come tho. She's going home soon," I told him.

Cheryl had worn out her welcome at the hospice and wouldn't let the other patients rest—and die—in peace. The nurses heavily sedated her, causing her to sleep through meals. When she woke up, she'd be hungry and there was usually no food around. The staff would bring her a plate, but the food would be cold. Then she'd have a temper tantrum by throwing things, cussing, and yelling. Sometimes she took her tantrum on the road and showed out in the hallway. The hospice would call my brother. He would then call my mother to ask why she was giving everyone such a hard time.

She and I joked about there never being any food around or a microwave in her hospice unit.

"Folks come to hospice to die. Dead folks don't make noise," I said.

"Exactly. Dead folks don't eat either," she replied.

"And dead folks don't ask for hot food."

That evening, while my mother was in hospice and I was in my third week of radiation therapy, was the first time in my forty-two years that I'd ever spoken to both of my parents at the same time. We were making new, happy memories. Their conversation was Blackity Black, hilarious, carefree, vulgar, straight ignant, incoherent at times, loving—the banter of two old friends who shared a child and a history without judgment. Cheryl had had enough bad customer service at the hospice and was going home. Surely, she wasn't at death's door. But even in that moment, I knew that conversation with my parents was special, something I would look back on and savor.

Tuesday, February 16, 2021

Last week, I had my second cancer dream. I dreamt that I had a Black doctor and that he was showing me images of my left breast with small dots of cancer cells or tumors emanating from my nipple all the way to the outside of my breast. "The radiation isn't working," he told me.

A friend recently asked me if I am "still hopeful." It was such an odd question. I certainly had many reasons to be hopeful. I'd had a lumpectomy. My surgeon had removed the tumor and six lymph nodes. The amount of cancer cells found in two of my lymph nodes was so small that their presence could not be detected on imaging tests and did not affect the staging of my stage 1B breast cancer. My MammaPrint score was low, so my oncologist said I didn't have to undergo chemo. I only had to undergo almost six weeks of daily radiation treatments, with weekends off, and ten years of getting Lupron shots monthly and taking anastrozole pills daily. I was coming out on the other side. But the truth is that I am afraid to be hopeful. Or rather, I am cautiously optimistic. For now. I'm afraid that I will die from breast cancer—maybe not this time, but eventually. I fear that it will come back, and the doctors won't catch it early enough. That I won't be as lucky next time.

I'm afraid to say I am "cancer free" because such a statement makes me feel like a fraud; because there might be lone cancer cells floating throughout my body that I do not yet know about. When I researched disability insurance, I learned that cancer is considered a permanent disease. When I looked up appointments for the COVID vaccine, cancer was the first listed qualifying medical condition. The two categories listed for cancer were "current" and "in remission." Even after years of hormone therapy and being "cancer free," the cancer can return. Studies have shown breast cancer can return as many as twenty years later, although the risk of recurrence is greatest in the first two years after diagnosis.

I am the president and ambassador of the performative happiness and positivity club. I'm often described as bubbly, happy, and positive—even under the worst, tear-inducing circumstances. I'm not superhuman or a Strong Black Woman. I simply don't have the luxury of falling apart because my bills still need to be paid, I still need a place to live, and my dog still needs his expensive food. The truth is that I am a magician and wear a happiness mask. Even when I share the facts of my life, I'm not really telling the truth. Even when I am smiling, I'm not always happy.

Taking off my mask requires me to manage others' judgments, fears, and projections. Baring my emotions entails trusting that others are able and willing to support me. When my friend asked if I was "still hopeful" after my breast cancer diagnosis and surgery, I could have told her the truth: that I was scared. But her question implied that *she* was not hopeful. I didn't have enough hope or strength for the both of us. Instead, I gave her an enthusiastic "Yes," uttered some Iyanla Vanzant–Maya Angelou words of wisdom, and changed the subject.

Tuesday, February 16, 2021

I talked to Cheryl twice today. The second time we spoke, she kept saying, "I'm so tired." She has been saying this more frequently these days.

"Sing to me," I told her. Her singing was the most natural, effortless, vulnerable thing she could do in that moment. A way for us to be close when she didn't feel like doing much else. She sang part of the gospel song, "I Won't Complain." The heaviness of her soprano voice and the lyrics said what we could not.

And then she turned to the topic of my non-existent love life. Although my mother is a lot better at being honest about her feelings, we share the tendency of abruptly switching from the heartbreaking to the lighthearted.

"When you gon get a boyfriend?" she asked me.

"Men are too much trouble, and I can't find a good one no how," I told her.

"You should have a part-time boyfriend," she offered. Admittedly, a part-time boyfriend might be easier to find.

"No, thank you," I replied.

We continued talking as I slathered conditioner throughout my unwashed hair. I'd planned to cover my hair with a shower cap for a half hour so the conditioner could penetrate my dehydrated strands before shampooing it.

"I'm thinkin' bout cutting my hair," I told her. "It's so much damn work and it has dried out even more since I started radiation."

I told her about my wash-day woes of my hair getting tangled when it's wet and me having to cut the knots out. I explained the new hair washing technique I planned to try that night: twisting my hair and then washing it with the twists in.

"Yea, that's too much work," she said. "You should just go get it done every two weeks." I only go to salons once a year to get a trim after giving myself several bad haircuts throughout the year. On a good day, I don't have the patience to spend hours in small, crowded places. COVID has made me even less inclined to do so. Cheryl, on the other hand, doesn't believe in DIY beauty routines. She is a connoisseur of lacefront wigs, professionally installed eyelashes, and manicures.

Cheryl and I are so different in how we pamper ourselves that one might think I'm disinterested in the feminine arts of hair, nails, and makeup. For the most part, I am. I wear my hair in a natural hairstyle, rotating between an afro, updo puff, or twist out. I can count the number of times on one hand that I've worn a weave and I've only worn a wig once. I've never worn false eyelashes, and only know how to apply mascara to my top lashes. I've never applied my own eyeliner, due to my poor eyesight and even poorer hand-eye coordination. I get a manicure and pedicure once or twice a year—including before trips so that my crusty feet don't embarrass me when I take my shoes off at the airport. It's not that I hate beauty routines. I just never fully recovered from my days growing up in the Pentecostal church, where it was a sin for women to wear makeup.

I do have one rebellion: a bold lip. I love a good lipstick or gloss—reds, purples, wines and berries, neutral browns, and mauves. Anything to add pizzazz to my face and dress up any outfit without doing too much. I once owned over seventy tubes of lipstick and gloss, but I've since stopped counting. If I had as much money in my bank account as I do Beauty Insider points at Sephora, I'd quit my job and travel for a year or two. However, a bold lip was not going to rescue my parched, uncooperative hair. Cheryl had a point, but I ignored her suggestion to go to the salon. I gave myself two haircuts within the next few weeks.

Saturday, February 20, 2021

I dreamt about Granny and Cheryl last night. In the first part of the dream, Granny was in the hospital, in room 310 on the right side of the hallway. When I returned to her room, she had gotten out of bed and was walking slowly. She was so slow and unsteady I thought she might fall. Then she was sitting on the bed. In the dream, I was thinking about her fever and sepsis, which she died from in real life. In the dream, Granny and I never spoke to one another or a doctor.

Then the dream changed to Cheryl being in the hospital. She struggled to talk, intermittently puffing out instructions to me. The COPD had caused her lungs to fill with fluid and her breathing was labored.

"When they send the money, make sure they send it every week," Cheryl told me.

"Okay, like an annuity," I replied.

I don't know who was supposed to send money or for what purpose they were sending it. Perhaps she was referring to the payment of a life insurance premium. The issue of Cheryl's life insurance was a running joke. While clean, she'd make regular monthly payments on a couple of policies that paid enough to cover her funeral expenses and have money left over for my brother and his children. Of course, the payout was contingent on her living for at least two years after the policy was issued—a clock that was constantly restarting. As soon as she went on a drug binge, she'd stop making payments and the policies would lapse. "You have a lot of money, so you can pay for my funeral," she would always tell me. I tried to convince her that I didn't have a lot of money, to no avail. I eventually lost track of when she was and wasn't insured.

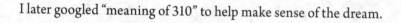

I later googled "meaning of 310" to help make sense of the dream.

1. Seeing 310 a lot reminds you to take better care of your financial life. It is a good sign for you to remember to invest, better organize your spending or spend less, and prioritize money for the future. Energies of wealth are close to you when you are seeing this number.[*]

2. The number 310 transmits energies of: intuition, wisdom, abundance, business, and efficiency. It brings the message for you to trust your angels and stop being afraid of the changes in your life, as they are beneficial for you.[†]

3. It may be that the angels are trying to tell you that, despite any bad moment, they are at your side and the good phase will come soon.[‡]

---

[*] "310 Angel Number–Meaning and Symbolism." Accessed June 10, 2021. https://angel number.org/310-angel-number/.

[†] Ibid.

[‡] Ibid.

4. Angel number 310 represents healing. It can be related to health, but it can also mean emotional and spiritual healing.[*]

5. If you have been going through a bad time with someone close to you, this angel number is a sign that it is time to begin making peace.

6. Begin the healing process and allow harmony and joy to enter your life. Let the past go and focus on the present and the future.[†]

When I was a child, someone called our house in the middle of the night and told Granny that her friend, an elder in our church, had passed away. I heard the conversation on our answering machine, which was in Granny's adjoining bedroom and sometimes recorded long portions of conversations even after we had answered the phone. At some point, I fell back to sleep. When I awoke and asked Granny about the phone call, she said it hadn't occurred. No one had called to tell us about Elder Harris's death. He was still alive, battling cancer, and the conversation I had heard was a dream. A few hours later, his wife called to tell Granny that Elder Harris had passed away at home.

    Dreams are God's and our ancestors' way of communicating with us. They foretell the future and have special meanings. Whenever Granny had a dream, she would try to decipher its meaning using the dream interpretation book she kept in her nightstand drawer. She'd sometimes go to the bodega around the corner to play the numbers she'd seen in her dreams, or she'd use those numbers to play the Lotto

---

[*] "310 Angel Number—Meaning and Symbolism." Accessed June 11, 2021. https://angel numbersmeaning.com/310-angel-number/.

[†] Ibid.

at the drugstore. Granny never won more than a few hundred dollars at a time, but every bit of money counted. Dreams contain messages; you just need to pay attention and heed the signs. Sometimes an ancestor's presence in the dream is the warning. "Whenever Ma'Dear comes to me in a dream, something's gonna happen," Granny would always say about dreams involving her mother.

I began cataloging my dreams after Granny passed away. The dreams she appeared in soothed me and made me feel more connected to her. I always dream about Granny when I need or miss her most, as if she can feel my spirit calling out to hers in another world. When I reviewed the dreams I'd had since being diagnosed with breast cancer, I realized they were my way of unconsciously processing my health-related fears. Through my dreams, I'd also been wrestling with my double grief—grief for myself and for Cheryl.

Wednesday, February 24, 2021

Voicemail: February 24, 2021 at 5:35 PM
Hey, Jodi, this Cheryl. They say it's bad. The nurse took two pictures of me and Uncle Bill gon send em to you. Okay? I love you. Call me later.

Despite the bad news my mother had just received, she still wanted me to see how fly she looked. For the last couple of days, Cheryl had complained about having trouble breathing. After hearing how she sounded on the phone, her doctor instructed her to go to the hospital. In addition to COPD, she now had pneumonia.

"I'm too pretty to die tonight," Cheryl told me when I spoke to her.

"Gurl, I know that's right!" I replied. "I guess that means you gon have to hold on."

I looked at the picture Uncle Bill texted me. In it, Cheryl has on a short, black wig with soft finger waves in it. Her hair reminds me of the cartoon character Betty Boop. Cheryl's deep brown face is smooth. She has thick, black false eyelashes on. An oxygen tube runs from her nose, wrapping around her ears on both sides. She's sitting upright with only her left arm and shoulder in a white sweater. Her left arm is on top of the bed railing, and she rests her face on her folded hand as she looks at the camera. An IV hookup is taped to her right hand. A tube is taped to her biceps and appears to be coming from underneath her arms and out of her shirt. Her short-sleeved shirt is high-collared and features black and white cats in various states on a gray background. Cheryl is wearing light blue, ribbed pants that look like they're made of a soft material, and a gold watch with a large, round, white face. In front of the watch is her hospital band, too big for her too-small wrist. Her nails are manicured. Her pinky nail on her left hand is painted with black polish and has a rhinestone near the cuticle. The nail on her ring finger is painted with a textured, iridescent silver polish. A large leather black bag sits between her legs, on top of the white sheet covering the lower half of her body. Cheryl is beautiful. Stylish. Vibrant. Death-defying. She doesn't look sick. Doesn't look like she's near death. She is too pretty to die tonight.

Wednesday, February 24, 2021

My mother asked me for a second time to call my father on three-way.

They talked about a mutual friend of theirs my father recently ran into.

"Call Vernon and let him know I'm in the hospital," my mother told my father.

"I sure will," he replied.

"I wanna go to church on Sunday," Cheryl said.

"You shouldn't be goin' to church. You know when the Holy Ghost hits, you ain't gon be able to stand six feet apart," my father explained. "And yo mask ain't gon be able to find you. The baby gon be playin' wit it on the floor." We all laughed at the image of Cheryl in church shoutin' her way out of her mask.

"Justin, do you have Facebook?" Cheryl asked.

"Uh huh," he responded. He and I are Facebook friends. Cheryl once sent me a friend request, but I declined it because I thought it was a fake page. The page only had a few friends, all of them men, and none of them were family members or people I recognized.

"I'm on there, too," my mother replied. "You want me to send you a picture?"

"A picture of what?" my father asked.

"I'ma send you a topless picture."

"No, Cheryl!" Justin yelled.

"Oh my gawd. Do not be sendin' nekkid pictures on the internet," I added.

"I'm just playin'" Cheryl added and started laughing. "Y'all know I wouldn't do nuthin' like that."

"No, we don't know," my father and I said in unison.

"I'm ya wife, nigga. I'm tryna get ya back." That's that OG level of female flirtation. In Cheryl's mind, she was the sexiest thing walking. And she had the receipts to prove it: she was never without a boyfriend or two, or some man willing to drop everything to come rescue her. She was confident, charismatic, and embraced her body. After her mastectomy, she chose not to undergo breast reconstruction. "My right tittie represents for all my titties, and whoever don't like it can go fuck themselves," she told me. Having only one breast, an A cup at that, did not stop her flow. During the Thanksgiving holiday in 2019, she told me about her unsuccessful attempt to seduce a guy.

"I had on a lil' sexy outfit and I was moving around on the bed," she said.

"What is you doing?" the guy asked Cheryl.

"I'm tryna have sex!"

Cheryl had no shame.

Cheryl grew tired of talking to my father and me.

"Jodi, take us out in prayer," my mother said.

"I don't know how to pray," I responded. That was a lie. After all, I was raised by Granny, the prayer warrior. But I felt too embarrassed to pray in front of my parents. I'd prayed in front of Granny before, but I'd never done in front of them. Growing up, prayer was often performative. She who prayed the loudest and most fervently and spoke in the most tongues was believed to be the sincerest. Loud, fervent, communal prayers were Granny's and the Pentecostal church's specialty. I love hearing a good, old-fashioned prayer. To feel the crescendo and power of the preacher's voice summoning God off His throne to do mighty works. A good prayer will bring you to tears. But I don't do prayers-on-demand and am not the loud, fervent, speaking-in-tongues type. For me, prayer is an act of humility and vulnerability. Prayer is intimate; private. Me telling God things I dare not utter aloud or in front of others; things I'm afraid to hope for out loud. What would I have prayed aloud that night on the phone with my parents? *Dear Jesus, please stretch out your nail-scarred hands and heal my mother and me. Heal our bodies and take away my mother's drug addiction.* A variation of the same prayer I'd prayed and written in my journals and letters to God since I was a child. Would God answer my prayers? Was I hoping for the impossible?

"Justin, go head and pray," my mother then directed my father.

"I pray for y'all all the time, but I prefer to pray in private," he responded. My father shared my prayer philosophy.

"Cheryl, why don't *you* pray?" I told her.

As she did with everyone else, she got right to the point with God. My father was first up on her prayer request list.

"Lawd, I want you to take that drinking spirit away from Justin." I tried not to laugh. The phone line got real quiet, as if Cheryl was waiting for a promise of sobriety from God or my father.

"Justin, are you still there?" I asked.

"I'm offended, but I'm still here," he said in a low breathy voice, as if the wind had been knocked out of him and he was trying to get back up.

"Lawd, pray for my chile. She not my only one, but she my chile," Cheryl clarified, in case God wasn't clear on the identity of all her progeny. "You know she got the same disease I got. Heal her and let her live."

"Yes, I gotta live. Cus don't none of my friends like Buster and they ain't gon wanna take care of him if I die," I added.

"Lawd, not Buster," my father added.

"Yes Lawd, heal my chile so she can continue taking care of Buster," Cheryl added to her prayer.

Cheryl called me early the next morning.

"I really enjoyed talking to you and ya daddy last night," she said. She sounded so happy and giddy, like a schoolgirl who had spoken to her crush. She mentioned that conversation several more times over the next couple of weeks. It was one of the last happy memories she'd make before she, too, became a memory.

Early March 2021

Shortly after my radiation treatments ended, I dreamt about Cheryl and Granny. In the dream, I said, "I want my mother." I don't know who I was talking to in the dream, but then Granny and Cheryl appeared. The three of us were in my childhood bedroom and I was lying on my back in the bed. Cheryl was seated or kneeling on my left side and Granny was on my right.

"I know I couldn't have been giving birth," I said to a friend a few days later. I'd never wanted to have children and my medically induced menopause from monthly Lupron shots helped ensure I never would.

"Well, what are you currently giving birth to now?" she asked.

I remained quiet.

"Your book. You're working on your book."

"I guess," I replied. Could the dream's meaning have been that simple? Throughout my treatment, I'd continued working on essays for my book about grief. Could it be that Granny and Cheryl were helping me to finish this book? Or could it be that they were both with me in spirit, helping me through the scariest time of my life. Although radiation was over and I'd started hormone therapy, I still had a lot of anxiety about the possibility of the cancer coming back. The constant updates from the numerous Facebook cancer groups I was in and the long list of possible side effects from the Lupron and anastrozole I was taking kept me on edge. I was afraid to do anything. Afraid to resume my job search for fear that the cancer would return soon after I started at a new job. Afraid to move to another city or state, away from my friends and medical team. I had never uttered the words "I need my mother" or "I want my mother" because Cheryl and I didn't have that kind of relationship. She'd been absent from so much of my life, unreliable and unavailable even when she was reachable. It was Granny, not Cheryl, who had raised me and cared for me when I was sick. But dreams have a way of helping us work out our subconscious fears and desires. Maybe deep down inside, I really wanted my mother. My fears had invaded my dreams and my two mothers, one still living and one dead, had come to comfort me.

Early March 2021

My cousin Lisa had a dream about Cheryl. In the dream, Lisa, Aunt Chris, and Granny were standing in Aunt Chris's kitchen. Cheryl was lying in a bed, facing the wall.

"What's wrong with Cheryl?" Lisa asked.

"Nothing's wrong with her. She's just tired and ready to go home," Granny replied. "They even have a bed for her."

I think the process of dying, rather than what happens after you die, is the scariest part about death. I learned this while Granny was dying. My prayers changed over the course of her thirty-day hospital stay. For weeks, I asked God to heal her and let her come home. By day twenty-nine, after watching tubes emanate from Granny's mouth, swollen hands, and various other places on her pain-racked body, I simply asked God to comfort her. "Let Your will be done," was my final prayer before she passed away.

Cheryl also knew that dying was not easy. That it could be ugly, prolonged, painful, lonely. She knew this so deeply that she had a death prayer.

"I asked God not to let me be in pain and not to let me be alone," she used to say. She prayed for this up to the very end.

Wednesday, March 10, 2021

Cheryl called me early that morning as I shook off sleep and stumbled to the bathroom.

"Jodi, can you help me write a book about my life?" she asked. She had launched right into her request without any salutations or small talk. She was amped up, as if she had been awake for hours. There was a sense of urgency in her voice.

"You wanna write a book?" I asked. She had never expressed an interest in writing; nor had she been interested in mine. I once sent her links to essays I'd written, but I doubt she read them because she never mentioned them.

"Yeah. I think my story could really help a lot of women. My addiction, my cancer, my hookin', things I been through."

And then we got cut off. I figured it was her ghetto phone acting up again. It had a tendency of hanging up without warning. I had just finished five and a half weeks of radiation treatment a couple of days prior and was relieved to not have to wake up so early. I crawled back into bed, thinking I'd just talk to Cheryl later.

Later that day, Cheryl asked my brother for $400. He was the representative payee for her disability checks and gave her money as needed. She told him she needed the money because she wanted to open a bank account. She told a friend she was going out to eat with someone. Cheryl left my brother's house and never came back home. My calls and texts to her went unanswered.

Tuesday, March 16, 2021

Cheryl called and updated me on what she'd been doing since she left my brother's house. First, she went to her usual spot and got high.

"I got scared so I hid in a closet," she told me.

"Why were you scared?"

"Because I knew I was too sick to be in a dope house and didn't wanna die there," she said. "I called my friend and he got me a motel room."

I didn't bother to ask why she had left my brother's house to get high. I knew why. The pull of her addiction was stronger than her willpower. Because she usually relapsed at the two-month sobriety mark. Because she'd been an addict for over forty years. Asking an addict why she got high is like asking why I keep drinking Coca-Cola or why a runner hits the pavement. On that Tuesday morning, sitting up in my bed, I wasn't looking for an explanation about why she hadn't or couldn't make better choices. I was just glad she was safe and wanted her to know I loved her.

"Well, at least you were only gone for a couple of days. Your binges usually last weeks at a time," I told her.

"I guess you're right. Progress, not perfection," she said.

"I'm so tired. I'm tired of fighting," Cheryl said. She was telling me about the oncology appointment she'd gone to since leaving my brother's house. "My oncologist said there's nothing else they can do. I asked him, 'What changed from three weeks ago?'"

Since being discharged from the hospital three weeks ago, nurses began coming to my brother's house to drain the fluid from her lungs through a tube they'd inserted while she was hospitalized. She also used a portable oxygen tank at home, which my brother had brought to her at the motel. Cheryl's oncologist had suggested that she start chemotherapy. According to Cheryl, her oncologist had believed the chemo would help decrease the build-up of fluid in her lungs.

"Sometimes cancer progresses just that fast," Cheryl's doctor told her.

"I asked him, 'Am I dying?' He said yes."

"Listen, we all gon die someday. You ain't goin' nowhere," I told her. I knew this was a lie and a useless platitude. But I didn't know what else to say.

"Yeah, we all gon die. But I'm gon die sooner rather than later," she replied. I remained silent.

Her oncologist wanted her to go into hospice immediately, but she planned to go stay with friends in Miami.

"How you gon get there?" I asked. I doubted she had the strength to make it from West Palm Beach to Miami.

"My friend's gonna drive me," she told me.

"After my appointment, I went to fill my prescription for my pain pills. I thought about taking the whole bottle and just going to sleep. But I wanna see Momma again. And I know if I kill myself, I'ma go to hell and won't be able to see her."

"Granny used to always say, 'God forgives everything except blasphemy and self-murder,'" I added.

"And I also didn't think anyone would find me, since I'm here alone," she said.

Even after a lifetime of drug use, she held on to her religious beliefs that suicide was a sin for which God would punish her and that we see our loved ones in the afterlife. She wanted to see Granny so badly that she was willing to prolong her own life, even if it meant facing her fear of pain and the unknown. Over the last few months, Cheryl often talked about how much she missed Granny. It was a longing and grief we had not been able to share when Granny passed away almost ten years prior.

"I wish Momma was here now," Cheryl had told me a few weeks ago.

"Me too," I answered.

Granny's faith in God was so sure, so strong, that you just knew her prayers would go straight to God and make everything alright. Her God-gon-work-it-all-out perspective on life, even the mere memory of it, was comforting and made my heart ache at the same time.

"What do you think she'd say if she were here?" Cheryl asked.

"She'd shake her head at both of us having breast cancer at the same time," I replied. I then put on my best Preacher Granny voice. "Then she'd bust out her bottle of holy oil, spread it all over our foreheads until it dripped down into our eyes and yell out 'Repent and get saved!'" We both laughed.

"I'm tired," Cheryl said to me for a final time.

"Alright. Go take a nap and call me later."

"I love you," she said in her high-pitched sing-song voice.

"I love you, too."

Saturday, March 20, 2021

My cousin called me from Cheryl's phone that evening.

"Cheryl is real sick, but she wants to talk to you. Hold on," he said. My mother got on the phone.

"Jodi, I need to see your face. I don't wanna die alone in a motel room. I need to see your face. I don't wanna die alone in a motel room," she kept repeating while crying and gasping for air.

"You're not gonna be alone. He's gonna stay with you," I kept telling her. My voice mingled with our cousin's, who also tried to console her.

"I'm not gon leave you. I'ma take you to the hospital. I'm not gon leave you," he told her.

Cheryl sounded weak. Her high-pitched, reedy voice sounded so thin. I could hear the congestion from her fluid-filled lungs. I asked my cousin multiple questions, trying to figure out why and how Cheryl had left the motel room she was staying in and ended up at his house and then another motel. I was also trying to determine whether her acute sickness had been caused by the cancer or the fact that she'd just gotten high. The cause was probably a combination of the two.

Cheryl's call rattled me. I'd never heard her in such distress.

"I got her," my cousin told me. "I'ma take her to the hospital. I'll call you when she gets settled."

That was the last time I ever spoke to my mother on the telephone. After my cousin took her to the emergency room, she was placed in hospice. I'd just finished radiation treatment for my own breast cancer and was scheduled to return to work from a two-month medical leave of absence. I arrived in Florida a week later to see my mother for the last time.

Saturday, March 27, 2021

My brother picked me up from the airport and we drove straight to the hospice to see Cheryl. She was asleep when we arrived. She was so small in her hospital bed that she looked like a child.

My brother introduced me to the young male nurse with shoulder-length hair who came into her room. Prior to my arrival, my brother had instructed staff to stop giving Cheryl pain medication.

"Your mother groans and yells out all day," the nurse told us. "She's in pain."

"She always makes noises in her sleep," my brother tried to explain. "She never takes pain medication at home. She's never in pain."

"But she has cancer in her bones. She *should* be in pain," the nurse said.

I listened silently as I rubbed her forehead with my left hand and held her hand in my right. I did not interject because I did not know how Cheryl behaved on a regular basis. Before absconding several weeks prior, Cheryl had lived with my brother, and he usually took her to her medical appointments. This was my first time seeing her since Thanksgiving of 2019.

"She's been in hospice before and walked out," my brother said. "I just need y'all to get her to the point where I can take her home. I'm not gonna let her die in here."

On our way out of the unit that day, the nurse called my brother over to the nurse's station.

"I googled bone cancer. It's the most painful cancer," he said.

"I understand what you're saying, but Cheryl is not your ordinary cancer patient."

Sunday, March 28, 2021

"Cheryl, are you in pain?" I asked. My hand was on her back, and she was facing the wall in a fetal position.

"Yup," she replied.

"Okay. The doctors are gonna get you sumthin."

"What are they gonna give me?" she asked.

"I don't know." Based on the conversation my brother and I had with the social worker and Cheryl's doctor earlier that morning, I knew they'd be giving her morphine and Seroquel. If that combo did not ease her pain, her medical team would resume her usual diet of morphine for the pain and Ativan and Haldol to keep her calm. But I didn't tell Cheryl this because I didn't want her to protest or become upset. Although this three-medication combo was the best at managing her pain, it was going to make her almost comatose. I didn't want her to weigh being in pain against being awake.

The social worker had called me earlier that morning to ask if we were coming up to speak with Cheryl's doctor.

"Either your brother will have to allow us to give her pain medication and treat her symptoms while she is here, or he will have to take her home this afternoon with no pain medication," the social worker told me. It was a scare tactic. Cheryl was too sick, too fragile, and in too much pain to even move—let alone go home.

My brother picked me up from my hotel and we went to the hospice to meet with Cheryl's doctor and social worker.

They had asked Cheryl earlier if she was in pain.

"Stop asking me that question," Cheryl had replied with her usual dose of feistiness. They didn't know if her response meant, *It's obvious I'm in pain, so get me some drugs* or *I'd tell you if I were in pain, so leave me the hell alone.* My brother and I laughed.

"That's the Cheryl we know," he said.

"Sometimes we can hear her all the way out here," the social worker told us. We were sitting in a small room outside the unit where Cheryl was located, steps away from the visitors' sitting area.

Grief makes your mind run in all sorts of directions, trying to make sense of a loss that has finally arrived at your doorstep. Trying to stave off the inevitable. It was difficult for my brother to accept that Cheryl's condition had deteriorated so much that she was in constant pain. Her decline had seemed so sudden. However, he also feared that the morphine would speed up our mother's death—that once they kept her sedated, she'd stop eating, her organs would shut down, and she would waste away. He wasn't wrong about the apparent effects of sedating Cheryl. Dying, sedated patients in hospice do not eat or drink. She was smaller than when she'd entered hospice several days prior. My brother asked whether Cheryl could be transferred to another hospice unit or facility that would not require her to be given morphine.

"Cheryl belongs here," the doctor explained. "But we have to be able to treat her symptoms."

I asked the question I knew my brother wanted the answer to. "Can breast cancer progress so quickly that she'd be in constant pain now, even if she wasn't before?"

"Yes, particularly if the tumors have developed deeper in her bones and reached the nerve endings," her doctor replied.

The doctor explained the medications and dosages they'd given Cheryl.

"The morphine is the same amount we'd give a child, but because she's probably not even eighty pounds, it knocks her out," the doctor said.

"She usually doesn't like pain meds because she doesn't want to become addicted to them," my brother explained.

"At this point, it doesn't matter," the social worker replied.

Sunday, March 28, 2021

I wasn't sure Cheryl recognized me with my mask on.

"It's me. Jodi. Lemme pull my mask down so you can see my pretty face," I said to her. She and my brother laughed.

"I still got a big butt like you," I said. "Lemme give you a twirl." Cheryl laughed and looked at me as I turned completely around. She was usually much heavier and used to tell me, "My stomach is leadin' and my behind is followin'."

Cheryl looked me up and down from head to toe.

"I got me an afro puff. Do you wanna feel it?" She nodded yes. I walked over to her bed and leaned down. She smiled as she dug her fingers into my thick, coily hair. I don't remember her ever touching me so intimately.

I felt like a young child showing off for her mom. I knew we didn't have much time and I wanted us to soak up all of each other. I wanted Cheryl to remember me after she was gone. I wanted to remember her laughter, her hands, her touch.

I also wanted to reassure her that I was okay. That I was healthy.

Despite my assurances, Cheryl was never sure that I was alright. On February 18, 2021, she texted me:

> Jody Jody I need to talk to you I love you I feel like something is wrong I want you to tell me the truth what's really going on with your cancer please tell me please tell me

She'd also told my brother that she felt I wasn't telling her everything about my breast cancer. There had been nothing to tell, other than that my daily routine for five and a half weeks was: go to my 9 AM radiation appointment every weekday; buy breakfast; slather Aquaphor and aloe vera gel over my left breast, underarm, and collarbone—all irritated and burned black from the radiation; and then sleep until three or four in the afternoon because the treatments, though short, exhausted me.

Although I told my mother I had no other news to share, she was the only one who suspected that the face I was showing the world was a mask. Perhaps she knew this because a mother always knows her child, or because she'd already walked the same path as me.

When Cheryl and I had talked on March 16th, while she was staying in the motel room, she told me that she'd sat in her own urine for forty-eight hours because she was too weak to get up.

"My friend came and washed me up, got me dressed, and carried me to the car so we could go to my oncology appointment," she explained. "I hope you're not going through this. I hope you never go through this."

There was nothing more to tell, other than my fears about the future. But I kept those to myself. Cheryl had her own fears to face.

"I'm scared the chemo's not workin'. My markers ain't goin' down," she'd told me a few months earlier. Her voice was full of anxiety.

"So, they'll just try a new medication," I told her.

She changed the topic of the conversation.

Sunday, March 28, 2021

People often see or ask for their dead mothers when they are dying. Some believe that our ancestors and family members come to accompany us to the afterlife. During Granny's final hospitalization, she began talking to her mother. Ma'Dear had come for her. Granny died a month later.

"I want my momma," Cheryl told me as I sat beside her bed.

"You want your momma?" I asked, to ensure I'd heard her correctly.

"Yea." I did not answer. I did not bother to tell her Granny was dead.

"Where is my momma?" Cheryl asked me several minutes later in an agitated tone.

"I don't know. But wherever she is, tell her to stay put cus I ain't ready to see her yet."

Monday, March 29, 2021

I called my father when I got back to my hotel room that night.

"I've been in town since Saturday, but I've been so busy I didn't have time to call you," I told him. "Cheryl is in hospice. It's not looking good. You need to go visit her tomorrow."

He and my younger sister visited Cheryl the next day and sat with her for a couple of hours. When I arrived, they came to the lobby to meet me. I hugged them both.

"Lil sis, lemme steal Daddy because this will be the last time I have both of my parents in the same room."

"I understand. I'ma wait in the car."

After the security guard wrote down my name and took my temperature, my father and I walked to my mother's room. She was much more sedated than she'd been in the past few days and wasn't responsive.

"I love you, Cheryl," I told her.

"This is the first time we've all been together since I was a baby," I told my father.

"Yup, and when we all talked on the phone that time, that was the first time we'd ever done that."

We didn't say much else during our visit. We knew the end was near.

Tuesday, March 30, 2021

When I went up to visit Cheryl, there was a horrible stench that got stronger as I neared her room. It smelled like a mixture of feces, vomit, and something rotting. *Ain't nobody gon clean that up?* I thought. When I arrived at Cheryl's door, I could tell the smell, thankfully, wasn't coming from her room. When I exited Cheryl's room later on, I saw a man pushing a gurney with a royal blue body bag on top of it. A white man holding a small dog stood across from the room next to Cheryl's, looking after the gurney as it rolled out of the unit and into the empty, skylight-covered sitting area.

"I'm so sorry. Was that your loved one?" I asked him.

"No," he replied. He was just being nosy like me. The gurney was our reminder that people do not leave hospice alive. Thinking back to the foul odor, I remembered the staff's instructions to my brother and me a few days earlier. *Let us know which funeral home you'll be using, because we do not have a morgue on site.*

Wednesday, March 31, 2021

I usually watched part of the Derek Chauvin trial each day before visiting Cheryl. That day, Charles McMillian was the star witness. He was one of the bystanders who saw Derek Chauvin murder George Floyd by kneeling on Mr. Floyd's neck for 9 minutes and 29 seconds. Erin Eldridge, Minnesota Assistant Attorney General, showed Mr. McMillian a video of police officers attempting to place Mr. Floyd into a squad car and then onto the ground outside the car. Mr. Floyd said "I can't breathe" multiple times and cried "Momma" seven times. Mr. McMillian sobbed as Mr. Floyd called out for his dead mother on the video. The video stopped and Ms. Eldridge gave Mr. McMillian a bottle of water and a few moments to compose himself. "Oh my God," Mr. McMillian said as he wept.

"I know this is difficult. Can you just explain sort of what you're feeling in this moment?" Ms. Eldridge asked Mr. McMillian.

"I feel helpless. I don't have a momma either. I understand him. My mom died June 25th," he replied as he tried to hold back his tears. His grief from the loss of his own mother intermingled with the grief of watching Mr. Floyd call out for his. Our mothers are our first place of refuge. To call out for one's dead mother is the pinnacle of helplessness and despair. It means you know that no one and nothing else can save you. Your screams are a prayer that Momma will move mountains and intervene, even from beyond this world. I wept as I watched Mr. McMillian testify. I wept for Mr. McMillian's pain—the pain of losing his mother; the pain of watching Mr. Floyd die; the pain of reliving both. I wept for my dying mother. I wept for Granny. Mr. McMillian and I wept for George Floyd. We wept for ourselves. We wept for the countless Black people murdered by police, most of whose killers will never be tried or convicted. The barbaric injustice of Mr. Floyd's death was like ripping a scab off our unhealed wounds. This is the nature of Black grief. Our personal and collective losses combined and compounded. Our daily lives are a reminder that your loss is my loss is our loss.

I eventually wiped my tears and steadied myself to go see my mother.

Wednesday, March 31, 2021

My father, his sister, and I arrived at the hospice to see Cheryl. Only two visitors were allowed in the room at a time because of COVID restrictions, so my father waited outside while my aunt and I went in first. We went through the normal front-desk routine and then headed to Cheryl's room. Once we entered Cheryl's room, the silence was so loud it startled me. She lay quiet, her mouth and eyes open. Her small chest no longer moved up and down struggling to take in air, as it normally did when we visited.

"I don't think she's breathing," I said to Aunt Dot.

"Check under her nose," she instructed me.

I placed my right index finger under Cheryl's nose to see if I felt any air coming out.

"I don't feel anything," I said.

"Check her wrist."

I grabbed Cheryl's right arm and placed my index and middle fingers on her wrist.

"Nothing," I said.

"Feel her neck."

Aunt Dot then began inspecting Cheryl's wrist for a pulse as I placed my fingers on her neck.

"Still nothing," I said.

I knew it was a hospice. I knew people came there to die. I knew patients typically died within five to seven days after admission. But my mind still did not want to believe the obvious.

"Go tell the nurse," Aunt Dot said.

I went to the nurse's station.

"I don't think my mother is breathing," I told the young nurse with the long hair. It felt less certain and less final than saying "I think my mother is dead." The nurse came into Cheryl's room.

"Yup, it doesn't look like it," he said in a flippant manner. "I'm sorry," he added as an afterthought, as if suddenly remembering that he must at least appear to be sympathetic. I expected him to follow up with, "Duh, you knew this would happen."

He took out a small flashlight and shined it in each of Cheryl's eyes. She did not move or react. Her pupils did not dilate.

The nurse left and returned with two women who wore face shields, masks, and pants and long-sleeved shirts that reminded me of hazmat suits.

One of the women took out her stethoscope and placed it on Cheryl's chest. She looked at me and shook her head.

"I'm so sorry for your loss. We're gonna call it at 4:34 PM."

Instead of having a funeral for Cheryl, friends and family gathered at a waterfront park and released pink balloons in her honor.

"I wanna thank everyone for coming today. We want Cheryl to know she was loved," I said to the group. Afterwards, my cousin prayed, and then my brother and others began speaking about their memories of my mother. I didn't give a speech that day. I was too afraid I'd burst into tears and not be able to find the right words. Anything I could say seemed insufficient. I've thought about her so much since her passing. This is what I want my mother to know:

Dear Cheryl,

We did not have an easy relationship. It was complicated. But none of that matters now. We were closer in the last six months of your life than we'd ever been. That was the time when I needed a mother the most. A time when I needed you most. A time when I was afraid and uncertain. Thank you.

I wish you had lived longer so that you could've gone to Paris like you wanted. I wish we'd had more time to get to know one another. I wish we could've been friends longer. Mother and daughter longer. We couldn't pack a lifetime of conversations and missed years into a few months, packed between surgeries and hospitalizations and cancer treatments and naps and drug binges.

My mother is dead. I sometimes walk around my apartment and say this out loud. It doesn't seem real. Although you were usually out in the street doing things you shouldn't be doing, I knew you were out there in the world somewhere—alive. And now you aren't.

You fought a lot of demons in your life. Masked a lot of pain. Gurl, you had more issues than *Vogue*. But you were mine. And you owned your shit. You lived and died on your own terms. May I be as brave as you.

I wondered what kind of ancestor you would be and then I got my answer. Shortly after I discovered the lump in my left breast in 2020, you texted me that I didn't have to go through this alone like you did; and that God had me the same way He had you. On October 18, 2021, a year and one day after your text, I remembered that message as a friend and I headed to the breast imaging center for my biopsy. While conducting an ultrasound, my first after having completed radiation seven months prior, the doctor found a small mass in my right breast. Thankfully, the mass was benign. On a day when I was afraid of what lay ahead, you reminded me that I'm not alone. No matter what happens, you're still here with me.

I'm glad Granny came for you. I know how much you missed her. Tell Granny, Aunt Jennye, and Aunt Lil I said, "Hey." You're in good company. I hope you're at peace now. Rest easy, Cheryl Ann. I love you.

8

The Ties That Bind

I am named after a dead child. A child I never knew. I have spent years trying to find meaning in my first name. It is undramatic and unproblematic. *Jodi.* It's short and only has two syllables. The most drama my name incites is questions about whether Jodi is spelled with an -i, an -ie, or a -y. It's the kind of name that makes people assume I'm white when they see it and then look surprised when they see me. The kind of name that doesn't ring ethnic bells on job applications. Jodi is a safe name.

When I was in college, an elderly neighbor stopped me one day as I passed his house.

"What's your real name?" he asked.

"Jodi," I replied. His question was odd because he and his family had known me for so long that they remembered my mother when she was pregnant with me.

"But what is Jodi short for?"

"Nothing. Jodi is my whole name."

"Oh. All this time I thought it was a nickname." Old Black folks sure know how to hurt your feelings to the white meat without even trying.

I once bought one of those souvenir cards that tells you the meaning of your name. I had hoped mine had a profound meaning, like faith, grace, victory, or God's favor. Instead, the card said *Jodi* means dog. I didn't even like dogs. In fact, they'd terrified me ever since our neighbor's dog Willie chased me from the backyard into my house when I was a kid.

Aunt Lil, Granny's younger sister, gave birth to a stillborn baby girl named Jodi. My mother Cheryl gave me the same name when I was born a year later. An Uber driver once told me that Jodi means *couple* in Nepali. "Two for the price of one," he said. Two children for the price of one. Or one child for the price of two. My name may be simple, but it has a profound meaning after all. You could say Jodi also means "a mother's second chance."

February 22, 1979
Bethune Cookman College
Daytona Beach, Florida

Dear Mom,

How is Jodi? Give her a kiss for me. Aunt Jennye told me that you were going to try to come down when I get out for spring break. Please do. I get out on March 16th and I am out for 2 weeks. I got the cards. Thank you.

My mother Cheryl was a nineteen-year-old college freshman and I was four and a half months old when she wrote this letter. Granny used to tell me that when my mother became pregnant with me at eighteen years old, Aunt Lil and Aunt Jennye wanted her to get an abortion because her pregnancy embarrassed them. My mother had been living with Aunt Jennye in Florida, where she also met my father and got pregnant with me. According to Granny, she told my mother to come to New York to give birth and that she would take care of me while my mother attended college. I don't know whether Aunt Lil and Aunt Jennye encouraged my mother to get an abortion or not, but she lived with Granny while she was pregnant and left me with Granny when she returned to school.

Granny proudly told anyone who'd listen that she brought me home from the hospital when I was thirty-one days old. Although my mother did not finish college, she remained in Florida and I remained with Granny. As parents do, Granny took me to the doctor for various and sundry reasons—routine check-ups, vaccinations, treatment for seizures I began having at six months old. She probably gave the doctors some variation of, "I'm temporarily caring for my granddaughter until her mother comes back for her." This worked for a while, until doctors and medical staff grew tired of her explanations and demanded official documentation showing that she had not stolen someone else's child. Granny eventually filed a petition in the Kings County Surrogate's Court to become my legal guardian. Although my mother never came back for me, Granny never adopted me. "I never adopted you or had your mother's rights terminated because she's still your mother. I'm believing God that she'll get off them drugs and get herself together one day," Granny would tell me. According to Granny, just because you *can* take someone's child doesn't mean you *should*. No matter how strung out on drugs and life my mother was, Granny still believed my mother deserved a chance to redeem herself. She did not want to replace my mother; nor did she feel it was appropriate for her to do so. Granny believed in the sanctity of the title *mother*. Whenever I was upset with Cheryl, Granny would say, "She's still your mother" or she'd quote Exodus 20:12: "Honor thy father and thy mother: that thy days may be long upon the land which the Lord thy God giveth thee." Once a mother, always a mother.

I saw a former neighbor at the local Pathmark supermarket several years ago. Her youngest daughter and I had been friends as children, and her older daughter used to babysit me and braid my hair. She filled me in on their lives: the status of her oldest granddaughter; younger grandchildren who had been born since I'd last seen her family; where they lived and what they did for a living.

"I don't even have to ask. I know you don't have no kids," she said.

"How do you know I don't have any kids?" I didn't have any, but I was offended that she hadn't at least asked.

"Because you always said: 1) your favorite color was purple; 2) you loved to read; and 3) you didn't want children."

"I said all of that at twelve years old?"

"Yup," she said.

She was right. All three of those things were true at twelve, and they are still true today. I have never felt a maternal urge or the anxiety of a ticking biological clock. The pain of pregnancy and childbirth never appealed to me; nor did they seem like a justifiable means to a justifiable end. When I was a child, I didn't play "house" with friends or pretend my dolls were two parents and children. Instead, my dolls and paper figures acted out stories I'd made up.

I don't remember how young I was when I first decided I did not want to be a mother. I don't remember articulating why either. I suspect that, subconsciously, not being raised by my parents greatly influenced this decision. I didn't trust that I would have the ability or support to be a good mother. My own father's absence and the scores of people I knew who'd been raised by single mothers, grandmothers, and aunts taught me that men are not reliable and do not stick around to raise their children. Although I saw women raising children, some of the women in my family had not raised their own children. And while I didn't always know the context and stories behind my family's legacy of maternal abandonment, my foremothers' choices and circumstances affected my beliefs about motherhood. They'd taught me that children were something you created by accident and just dropped off for other people to raise while you went off and lived your own life. I didn't see the sense in having children just to give them to other people. Although I'd initially viewed our circumstances as "abandonment," the reasons mothers and daughters in my family had been separated were far more complicated than I'd ever imagined. These *women* were far more complicated, more imperfect, and more deserving of grace.

My junior year of high school, Granny was in the hospital for a month. The hospital was across the street from my school, so I'd visit her every day before heading home. One of Granny's friends would come stay with me at night after she got off work. My guidance counselor called Granny in her hospital room and said her sisters, my Aunt Jennye and Aunt Lil, had called the school and told him that Granny was in the hospital and I was home alone. My guidance counselor also informed Granny that my aunts had begun making preparations for me to finish high school in Florida. They'd identified the high school I would attend and had inquired about the process for transferring my school records to Florida. Upon hearing this news, Granny signed herself out of the hospital against medical advice that day. Granny was bitter about that for a long time and stopped talking to my aunts for a while. In a letter Aunt Lil wrote me while I was in college, she said she didn't understand why Granny was angry with her. Thinking back, I don't know if Granny ever told my aunts that she knew they'd reported her to my school, tried to get custody of me, and planned to have me finish high school in Florida. I would imagine that my guidance counselor told them he'd spoken to Granny, but neither Granny nor my aunts ever mentioned discussing the issue.

I wonder if my aunts really thought they'd done the right thing. What they did was equivalent to calling the police or Children's Services on Granny to report her for child abandonment or neglect. What if I'd been taken from Granny—and them—and placed in foster care? What if Granny had been required to attend a court hearing to determine who should have custody of me? They could have handled matters differently: like coming up to stay with me while Granny was hospitalized or coordinating with Granny's friends to make sure I wasn't home alone. Instead, they were willing to rip me away from my home and the woman who had mothered me since I was born.

To my aunts, children were property, and possession determined motherhood. As with property, possession was nine-tenths of the law. A mother is whoever gets their hands on the child, genetics notwithstanding. Granny was always very protective of me in a way that seemed obsessive and paranoid. It's as if she was always on guard against the possibility of someone trying to take me away from her. Aunt Jennye and Aunt Lil's stunt proved that she had good reason to be cautious. In all my teenage naivete, however, I had attributed my aunts' behavior to their being overzealous, concerned family members. But that wasn't the whole story. I didn't know it at the time, but they'd already taken one child from Granny. She wasn't about to lose another.

Aunt Lil was my gossip buddy. I'd ease up to her and whisper in her ear, "I got some gossip for you." She'd laugh and I'd dish out the latest family drama I'd overheard from the adults—news she most likely already knew. She always called me "kid" and taught me how to play dominoes and the card game Tonk. She'd fuss at me and Aunt Jennye, my shopping buddy, whenever we snuck bags into the house and thought she hadn't noticed. Aunt Lil's voice reminded me of Granny's. I once woke up in Aunt Jennye's waterbed, thinking I'd heard Granny talking in the kitchen. After a few moments, I realized it was Aunt Lil's voice I'd heard and that Granny was still in New York.

Aunt Lil was a tough woman. She'd cuss you out with the quickness—even if you were a kid. She was light skinned, much lighter than her three siblings and everyone else in our family. She bestowed a special dispensation of cussin' on anyone who dared to call her "high yella." She wore many hats throughout her life: city councilwoman; accountant; director of a daycare center; a singer with a booming alto voice; and a pianist and choir director. She was the alto and Aunt Jennye had an operatic soprano voice. They used to sing in a local gospel group. Aunt Lil showed me that I could do and be whatever I wanted in life. When I started college, she used to write me and send me care packages. But she didn't live to see me graduate. Aunt Lil never had any more biological children after her first child, Jodi, was stillborn. But she later adopted my brother and a little boy who was a year older than me.

The thought of having children even terrifies me in my dreams. I recently dreamt that my friend Taylor and I went to a clinic in the neighborhood I grew up in. As we were leaving, a nurse followed us outside and told us I was pregnant. "Get it out! Get it out! I want an abortion now!" I yelled. Taylor and the nurse looked at me with wide eyes, as if it were strange for me to be so resolute, so quickly, about not wanting to keep my child. As if it was strange for me to not rejoice at the news of being with child. I was relieved when I awoke.

Although I knew my mother had spent a large part of her childhood in Florida being raised by Granny's sisters and mother, I wasn't sure why my mother had left Granny's care in New York. Granny told me my mother had moved to Florida after a bout with tuberculosis, a common illness in the 1960s. "The Florida air was better for her lungs," she said. After Granny's death, various family members told me that my mother had moved to Florida as a child because of behavioral problems. "Annie Lee was scared of your mother," more than one of them had told me. "She'd cut your grandmother's hair while she was asleep and Annie Lee would wake up with Cheryl standing over her."

While sifting through an old bag of papers and pictures after Granny died, I discovered a letter Aunt Jennye had written to her when my mother was ten years old. It was a five-page missive written on baby blue, lined paper with her initials JT in blue calligraphy on the upper right-hand corner of each page. Her letter stated, in part:

December 8, 1970
3:30 PM

Dear Annie,

. . . She is your child and I know you miss her, but you must know that this is a better environment for her than New York. She can walk to school alone, without the threat of being mugged. She can play in her own yard without the threat of being or becoming involved with street walking dope addicts.

Despite all of the problems you have had with her, she is doing very well in school, she loves school, she is *not* sick and *hasn't* been sick since the time she's been with us (from age 7–10). The only thing that happen[sic] is she broke her glasses the other day and I'll have to get more. All of Cheryl's sickness is in *your mind*. I honestly believe you should see a psychiatrist and try and get your problems work[sic] out before it is too late, because you know God works through doctors also . . .

So I decided the *only* way you'll take Cheryl back to New York before school closes is to *take me to court to do it. And Annie Lee* believe me *I am not Bluffing* you. I mean every *word*

of *it*. Remember, I work for Juvenile Court and the judge I'll
have to go before is my boss . . .

I want it to be on record that I did all I could to keep her
out of that awful city. I don't ever want Cheryl to choose
between us because she is your child. But I do believe and
I am sure the court will agree that you'll have to get yourself
together before it is too late . . .

It greaves[sic] me deeply to do this but if you intend to take
Cheryl back to that awful place, come prepared to get a court
order, because I've made up my mind and that is the only way
she'll leave Florida this time.

Your sister,
Jennye

Aunt Jennye wrote that my mother had been with her from age
seven to ten. I hadn't realized that my mother had moved to Florida
when she was so young. Aunt Jennye's letter didn't specifically mention my mother's behavioral problems or Granny's inability to disci-
pline her, but perhaps this was part of what she meant by "all of the
problems you have had with her."

I was angry when I read Aunt Jennye's letter. I was angry that
she felt she had the right to take Granny's child from her. Angry
that she viewed Granny as a lying mother, driven by Munchausen
syndrome by proxy, who needed to see a psychiatrist and whose child
needed protection from her. It occurred to me that perhaps Aunt Jennye and the rest of our family in Florida didn't know Granny as well
as they thought they did. Aunt Jennye wrote that Granny needed to
get herself together before it was too late, as if Granny were irrespon-
sible. However, Granny's diary from 1969 to 1970 revealed that she
worked at a clothing store in downtown Brooklyn. She'd told me she
used to work at the department store Abraham & Straus. She'd also

worked as an overnight caregiver for the sick and was studying to become a nurse's aide. I also read about her religious life and the village of church friends who loved and supported her—many of whom I'd heard Granny talk about over the years and had even met.

If Granny wanted custody of my mother, she would have to come to Florida and file a petition for custody in court—something that would take resources and money Granny didn't have. To reinforce Granny's powerlessness in the situation, Aunt Jennye reminded Granny that she was a secretary for a judge in juvenile court. She lorded her privilege over Granny.

The Aunt Jennye who'd written that letter to Granny eight years before I was born was not the same woman I knew. She was my favorite aunt and could do no wrong in my eyes. Aunt Jennye was the epitome of class and I was fascinated by how she carried herself. She walked and talked and moved as if she knew she was a very important person.

She was also the quintessential fabulous child-free auntie. I spent my summers either at her house or Aunt Lil's. She and I used to stay up late watching the Morton Downey, Jr. talk show while drinking cappuccinos topped with whipped cream and cinnamon. In the mornings, we'd sit on her screened porch in our robes, with our legs crossed, and drink tea and eat toast for breakfast.

She had scleroderma, an autoimmune disease that causes the skin and internal organs to harden and tighten. The disease affected her lungs, requiring her to use oxygen most of the time. Whenever she had a coughing fit, I'd yell, "Get it out! Get it out!" We'd laugh afterwards. Although she walked around with a portable oxygen tank, that didn't slow her down. She dressed up every day and lived her life with pizazz. She was a stylish lady. The kind of woman who had monogrammed stationery. She loved pretty clothes, wore rings on almost every one of her stiff, swollen fingers, and painted her toenails and fingernails with a copper-colored polish. White spots freckled her chocolate skin because she had vitiligo. She always wore a full face of Dermablend makeup and looked like she could've been a Fashion Fair model.

Aunt Jennye encouraged my love of school and reading. I read her copy of *Dune*, and all the Mary Higgins Clark novels on her bookshelves. She rewarded my good grades with shopping sprees at my favorite clothing store Jacobson's and other places. One of my favorite end-of-the year rewards was a pair of red, wire-rimmed glasses from JCPenney because I wanted red glasses like talk show host Sally Jessy Raphael's. Aunt Jennye also exposed me to role models, the most memorable of which was then-mayor Clara Williams. She took me to city hall several times to visit Mayor Williams, a Black woman who was Riviera Beach's first woman mayor.

Aunt Jennye never had any biological children of her own. But all the kids in our family, from my mother's generation and mine, loved her so much. My last phone conversation with Aunt Jennye was about my high school graduation ring. I sat on the floor of Granny's bedroom and told Aunt Jennye which ring I wanted and how much it cost. She bought it for me but didn't live long enough to see me wear it.

Granny's diary revealed that my aunts' lack of faith in her parenting ability and decisions had been an ongoing source of conflict between them and Granny for a long time. When she was alive, she told me she had moved back to Florida to care for her stepfather. Her diary entries support this. She wrote that she gave her friends her furniture and things to remember her by. She arrived by train on December 20, 1969. During her stay in Florida, she stayed with her mother, stepfather, and Aunt Lil, and my mother lived with Aunt Jennye.

December 25, 1969 (Christmas Day; a
year before Aunt Jennye's letter)

the children were making so much noise I had to finally get
up . . . Very depressed and lonely about many things Cheryl
is not being brought up right and I am very hurt over that But
God knows and he will give me what to do about it . . . the
Devil raging.

"The children" most likely referred to my mother, Aunt Chris and
Uncle Bill's three children, and my mother's other cousins. Reading
Granny's diary entry was like attending a family reunion. She didn't
mention what my mother got for Christmas or detail the children
opening their presents. I can imagine the number of gifts my mother
and her cousins received. When I was growing up, Aunt Chris and
Aunt Jennye were the Christmas queens. They went all out for the
holidays. When the Cabbage Patch Kids dolls came out in the eight-
ies, Aunt Jennye was one of thousands of people across the country
who stood in long lines for them.

January 6, 1970

Phone ring at 3:00. [My stepfather] passed to the great
beyond.
    Call Jennye. Spoke to Cheryl we had a few words because
she Jennye did not think I say the right thing.

January 8, 1970

Arose around 8:45 put my clothes in soak pack some of my
clothes in case I go back to Bklyn.
    Sit down to write Jennye.

We had a heated argument about Cheryl and what I must do with her.

Out for a walk to clear my head.

January 19, 1970

God knows and sees all things. I am going to wait until my change come. Lord touch me and guide me your way and how to act at all times in Jesus name.

January 28, 1970

Got my clothes ready for going to the school.

Cheryl call to ask me if I was coming tonight. Mother Dear took me over to Jennye at 7:00. Left for the school at 7:30. Talk to the teacher and [illegible] of the school. Found out somethings I needing to know. Came back. Gave her card. Stayed a while. Roosevelt drove me home by 9:00.

Granny went to my mother's school for parent-teacher night. I wondered what my mother's grades were like and what her teacher had told Granny. While I was growing up, Granny took open school night seriously. She proudly smiled when the teachers complimented me and her parenting and scolded me in front of the teachers if they gave her a bad report about me.

February 1, 1970

Cheryl had her birthday cake after dinner . . . Went for a drive near 5:15 then Cheryl went back to Jennye got suitcase out for clothes to New York.

Granny eventually returned to New York and my mother remained in Florida.

Aunt Jennye believed her middle-class background, suburban home, white-collar job as a secretary for a family court judge, and her status as a married woman made her a better parent. She believed that Granny's status as a poor, unwed mother living in a Brooklyn apartment in "the ghetto" made her a bad parent and undeserving of raising her own child. Aunt Jennye referred to New York as "that awful city" and "that awful place." She thought Florida was "a better environment" for my mother than New York because of her fears about the crime-ridden North and the heroin epidemic at that time. Aunt Jennye thought avoiding urban areas was the only way to avoid these social ills. Her views were consistent with social attitudes of the time about Black single mothers and northern urban areas, many of which were legitimized by the 1965 report *The Negro Family: The Case for National Action,* commonly called the Moynihan Report.

Written by then–Assistant Secretary of Labor Daniel Patrick Moynihan in President Lyndon B. Johnson's administration, the Moynihan Report criticized the Black family structure and out-of-wedlock births in the Black community. The Moynihan Report attributed the "tangle of pathology" in the Black community to its "disintegrating" family structures and increase of matriarchal families. It focused on the social ills of "urban ghettos" and "northern urban areas" like New York City, Chicago, Philadelphia, Detroit, and the District of Columbia.

The Moynihan Report contributed to the false sense of security Aunt Jennye and others had about being middle class by comparing the safety and success of middle-class Black people to the failures of working-class and poor Black people. The Moynihan Report noted: "The Negro family in the urban ghettos is crumbling. A middle-class group has managed to save itself, but for vast numbers of the unskilled, poorly educated city working class the fabric of conventional social relationships has all but disintegrated . . . So long as this situation persists, the cycle of poverty and disadvantage will continue to repeat itself." The report measured the impact of these "broken homes" by reviewing several social indicators, including the number of children born out of wedlock, the number of children and families who received public assistance under the AFDC program, unemployment rates, crime statistics among adults and juveniles, and narcotics usage. By focusing on the evils of the poverty- and crime-infested North, Aunt Jennye missed the dangers lurking in her own suburban backyard.

To be a Black woman who does not want children is often seen as abnormal in the Black community. A guy once flat-out asked me, "What's wrong with you?" when I told him I didn't want children. It's as if having children is the rent women pay for being alive and for choosing to be in heterosexual relationships. As if having children is as inevitable as getting your period.

Women often don't feel free enough to admit that we don't want children because we are so worried about being liked by men, loved ones, and society. We often feel the need to offer disclaimers so others don't think we're heartless monsters: "Kids are expensive," "I don't want to bring children into the world because it's a dumpster fire," or "I love children and have tons of nieces, nephews, and godchildren." All these things may be true, but "No" is a complete sentence. We don't need to justify our decision to not have children. That life choice is in the "nunya business" category.

Some of us hide our child-free aspirations from our partners. We string boyfriends and husbands along with "I'm not ready right now" and "Let's wait until later, when we're more established," hoping we can delay "later" until we reach menopause and our partner forgets all about having children. The anxiety caused by such dishonesty and the prospect of that baby bill coming due is too exhausting. It is far easier to live authentically.

Some have even told me, "You'd make a great mother because you took such good care of your grandmother." I loved Granny and would do it all over again. My answer to motherhood is still, "Nah, I'm good."

Crack addict. Criminal. Excuse-maker-in-chief. Not even a good enough mother to be called a bad one. This is how I had always viewed my mother. But I remember the first time I saw who she had been before she became any of these other things—the first time I saw her as a daughter. In 2013, a couple of years after Granny's death, I discovered a letter my mother had written to Granny when she was eleven. I was thirty-four years old when I read my mother's letter.

circa 1971

Dear Mom,

When am I going to come home? I just can't seem to fit in like they want me to. So when am I coming home? I think I can help you. I could get a job, you know.

Granny was living in New York and my mother was living in Florida with Aunt Jennye and the rest of our family. It hurt to picture my mother as a little girl, longing to come back home to Granny. In her childhood innocence, she thought she could help support herself and Granny. Someone must have told her Granny couldn't afford to take care of her.

As an adult, my mother and Granny had a strained relation- ship. I'd always thought it was because Granny was disappointed with how my mother's life had turned out and my mother felt guilty about having disappointed Granny. But my mother had her own disappointments.

After Granny developed Alzheimer's disease, one of her home attendants noticed that she was always agitated after speaking with my mother on the telephone. Granny and my mother usually spoke when I wasn't home, so I didn't know the nature of their conversations or why they upset Granny. One evening I overheard Granny talking to my mother and her friend, who was also sometimes her boyfriend.

"No, no that's not true. That's not true," Granny said into the phone. She seemed upset so I took the phone from her.

"You didn't tell Cheryl you loved her enough when she was a child," my mother's friend said, not realizing Granny was no longer on the phone.

"What are you talking about and what is wrong with you?" I asked him. My mother had apparently told this man about the woes of her childhood. I was annoyed that, at almost fifty years old, my mother hadn't gotten over her childhood issues of feeling unloved and abandoned by Granny, and that she thought trying to have this conversation with Granny made sense and would be productive. I was even more annoyed that she had enlisted the help of her friend in this mother-daughter intervention. It seemed as if my mother was trying to blame Granny for her choices and how her life had turned out. I was working and also caring for Granny. If I didn't have the luxury of taking a break to confront my mother about how she had failed me, then she would have to talk to Jesus about her unresolved issues with Granny.

"Cheryl, she has Alzheimer's disease. She's not going to remember this conversation tomorrow," I tried to explain.

Even after years of drug addiction and hard living, my mother was still that little girl who wanted to come back home to her mom. She was still that child who thought her mother had abandoned her and hadn't loved her enough. But too much time and memory had passed. Granny would never be able to give my mother the validation and explanations she sought.

Granny's Diary, December 2, 1969
(a year before Aunt Jennye's letter)

... left the house 9:10 to subway arrive at work 9:45 ... A fair day at the store. Got Cheryl and Kath coat and dresses was stop by the guard to check bags at 6:00. left the store at 6:30 for home

I first mentioned Aunt Jennye's letter to my mother several years ago. I wanted to provide her with some context about her childhood that no one, including Granny, had ever given her. I wanted her to know that Granny didn't abandon her, or at least not on purpose. I also wanted to ask her questions about Granny and our aunts.

"Our family is crazy," she said before changing the topic.

During the last few months of my mother's life, I mentioned Aunt Jennye's letter to her again. This time, she was in the mood to talk about her childhood.

"I remember Momma coming to pick me up from school one day," she told me. "It was cold. She brought a white coat for me to wear. We took the plane back to New York and I called Aunt Jennye from the airport."

I wondered if the white coat my mother wore back to New York is the same coat Granny wrote about in her diary. I notice that Granny only bought one coat and multiple dresses, presumably one dress for my mother and the other for my mother's cousin Kathi. My mother didn't mention that she knew she'd be leaving Florida that day. It seemed as if the trip had surprised her, as if Aunt Jennye and Granny had been in a custody dispute and Granny had sneaked her away. Perhaps Granny had allowed my mother to call Aunt Jennye from a pay phone at the airport so that she and the rest of the family wouldn't worry.

Over the years, my mother would occasionally mention her time in college. "I studied criminal justice," she would proudly tell me. When I was in high school, she was on an episode of the TV show *Cops*. Although Granny and I never caught the original episode or reruns, my Aunt Naomi saw it several times in Ohio. According to my mother, someone called the cops because she and her landlord had gotten into a fight. "He was tryna fuck me," my mother told me. She later complained that *Cops* didn't have the right to show her on TV because she never signed a release form. "The Supreme Court recently ruled that you can't show video footage of people on TV without their signed consent," she told me as we sat outside on Aunt Jennye's car. She was an addict with a long rap sheet who'd wanted to major in criminal justice and kept track of court decisions. She would've made a great attorney in another life.

I wondered how my mother had gone from being a college student with a four-year scholarship to a life of drugs. Her answer to that question frequently changed.

"I used to work down there at the courthouse where Aunt Jennye worked," she said more than once. "They used to have parties and there would be drugs there. That's how I started usin'."

On other occasions, she told me that she'd started using with her best friend.

"My best friend's father was a dope dealer," she explained. "I was interning at the courthouse. She'd come pick me up after work and we'd go to her house."

She'd been using for so long that she may not have remembered how she got started. Granny had always insisted that my mother began using drugs earlier than she admitted to. Whatever the precise details of her drug origin story were, the common threads were that she began using while in college; she had easy access to drugs; and she'd been introduced to them by people she knew. My mother never finished college and battled her addiction for nearly forty years with intermittent bouts of sobriety. Aunt Jennye's middle-class values didn't save my mother.

I think about what my mother could have done and been. I think about what her life might have looked like if Granny had raised her, but people and life outcomes aren't interchangeable or predictable. So much of my identity and Granny's parenting relied upon me being the opposite of who my mother had become. Granny's strictness, overprotection, investment in my life and well-being—her every effort was directed towards ensuring I didn't get pregnant before marriage, finished college and law school, and didn't become a drug addict. "You're not going to turn out like your mother," Granny would tell me. That was as much my mantra as it was hers. I don't drink alcohol more than once or twice a year, if that. When I was a kid, I took a sip from the can of Budweiser beer my mother left in the car with me when we made a quick stop at someone's house. I didn't like how it tasted so I never drank beer again. I don't smoke and I've never tried marijuana or drugs. A friend and I tried smoking one of her mother's cigarettes in the hidden sanctuary of her bathroom once. We were thwarted by her upstairs neighbor, who smelled the smoke through the air shaft and came down to ask if everything was alright. My abstinence from alcohol and other substances isn't based on a belief about their immorality. I just didn't want to end up like my mother.

I'm sure my mother never planned to become addicted to drugs. No one ever does.

When Granny told me her grandmother had raised her, I assumed her grandmother lived with Granny, her siblings, and their mother and stepfather. It wasn't until several years after Granny's death that I learned this wasn't the case.

During a telephone conversation with Uncle Bill, I mentioned Granny's long-standing accusations that their stepfather had sexually abused her when she was twelve years old. She told me on numerous occasions that it happened when she came home at night after cleaning white people's homes, a job she'd gotten by lying and saying she was older.

"When I came home, everyone else in the house would be asleep. My stepfather would come into my room and touch me," she'd say.

"It probably did happen," Uncle Bill told me that day on the phone.

"One day, our grandmother came to our house and she was real mad. She said, 'I'm taking my girls with me,' and began packing their things. I didn't know what happened. I was a child so the grown folks wouldn't talk around me, but I knew it must've been bad. She took my sisters to live with her and left me with our mother. And she told our stepfather, 'You betta not say a word to them.'"

This was the most I'd ever heard anyone in our family say about Granny's allegations against her stepfather. Our family never talked about what happened after Granny came forward. I'd heard family members say, or imply, that Granny had lied about the abuse. Granny had been vindicated. Uncle Bill's story supported her never-changing narrative.

This was the first time I'd ever heard that Granny's grandmother had her own house and had taken Granny and her sisters to live with her. Granny's grandmother had saved, protected, and loved her.

Granny always said her teacher and grandmother were the only people who believed her, which meant that her mother, whom everyone affectionately called Ma'Dear, did not believe her. I wonder what conversations Granny had with her mother about the abuse. Did Ma'Dear call her a liar to her face or did she call Granny a liar through her inaction? Ma'Dear stayed married. She chose her husband over her child. Granny didn't talk much about how her abuse affected her relationship with her mother, but it must have impacted their relationship in some way.

Granny returned to Florida years later, in the 1970s, to care for Ma'Dear when she was dying of breast cancer.

"I didn't think you'd come," Ma'Dear said.

"I came home for my stepfather. Why wouldn't I come for you?" Granny replied.

For Granny, being a daughter meant forgiveness, care, and fulfilling one's familial obligation—even if your mother has not always cared for and protected you. I can see how Granny's relationship with her mother and grandmother shaped her own notions of motherhood by the time I was born. For Granny, *mother* came to mean *fierce protector*.

My oncologist and breast surgeon asked if I wanted children. If I did, I'd need to explore the option of freezing my eggs—especially because my treatment for the next ten years would induce menopause.

Each time doctors asked the question, I responded with a quick "No."

"Wow. You're so certain," my oncologist said. I've never been more certain about anything in my life.

My decision to remain child-free reduced my pool of dating prospects. When dating or creating online dating profiles, I made sure to let men know that motherhood was not on my to-do list. I didn't respond to men whose profiles indicated they wanted (or had) children. However, some fathers and aspiring fathers still messaged me. After I'd messaged back and forth with one guy, he finally admitted that he wanted children—five children to be exact. I blocked him without further comment. I was clear in my profile and I wasn't going to change my mind. It amazed me that he talked so cavalierly about wanting that many children, considering that he'd never have to give birth.

There were a few guys who tried to negotiate and get me to agree to have one or two children, as if giving birth to and mothering fewer children was a de minimis inconvenience and reasonable compromise. My favorites are the men who have children but are impressed and relieved when I tell them I don't have children. "If you don't want to date a woman with kids, what makes you think I'd want to date a man with kids?" I always ask. That one always stumps them. What's good for the child-free goose is good for the gander. I scoff at the men who are bewildered that I don't want children, but barely have a relationship with their own kids. The jokes write themselves.

Granny, my mother, and I were all sexually abused as children. When I was in my thirties, my mother told me that a man Granny had dated abused her. My mother said I was the first person she'd ever told. Her revelation created a new sadness in me. I thought about all the ways her secret had worn her down, and all the ways she had tried to ignore, mask, and overcome the effects of her abuse. Had she remained in New York with Granny, the abuse probably would have continued until the perpetrator and Granny broke up. I saw the perpetrator at a funeral several years after Granny passed away. I'd heard Granny talk about him over the years, but I didn't remember ever meeting him. When someone pointed him out to me, I glared at him from a distance. I was sure he didn't know who I was, but I wondered if he remembered my mother. I also wondered how many other children he'd violated over the years.

My mother and I did not share our stories of sexual abuse with one another until I was in my thirties. I didn't tell Granny about my abuse until I was in my twenties, and my mother never got a chance to tell Granny about hers at all. I thought about how healing and freeing it might have been for all three of us to share the secret that bound us all.

My friend Janine and I recently had a conversation about our experiences being bullied as children. "Not being able to protect my child is one of my biggest fears about being a parent," I told her. So much of my decision to not have children was subconsciously rooted in fear. Fear of not being able to protect them from bullies and predators. Three generations of women in my family were sexually abused. Three generations of women spent a lifetime dealing with the effects of that abuse. Three generations of women fought their own battles of survival without the support of their mothers. No matter how hard parents try, children aren't safe in this world—especially girls. The cycle stops with me.

Granny proved Aunt Jennye and others wrong. She loved taking care of children and being a mother, and she was great at both. After Granny passed away, I found her study notes from a childhood education class she took at Bank Street College of Education in New York City. Before and after I was born, she worked in daycares and babysat children in her home. She also took care of foster children. I discovered a list she'd made of every foster child she ever cared for. Beside each name, she noted the dates they'd been in her care. I also found a handwritten draft of a letter she'd written to the birth mother of one of her foster children. The mother had recently regained custody of her daughter. In the letter, Granny doled out parenting advice and told the mom how much she and I missed her daughter. I wondered about Granny's foster children: how their lives had turned out and whether they remembered Granny. I also saw Granny's redemption. She'd done for me and so many other children what she had not been able to do for my mother. She poured all her loss, regrets, and lessons into mothering us. When she loved her foster kids and me, she chose motherhood on purpose. The one thing I know for sure is that my grandmother loved me. She chose me on purpose and loved me assiduously. To know that kind of love, her love, is a beautiful blessing. To realize I'll never know that kind of love again breaks my heart.

Granny knew me well, even the parts of me I didn't discuss with her. She'd told me on several occasions that she knew I would never have children. She didn't guilt-trip me into motherhood like so many grandparents do with their "I want to have some grandchildren before I die" speeches. She didn't try to scare me into motherhood by telling me I'd regret not having children and wouldn't have anyone to care for me when I'm old. Instead, she championed my educational and professional goals. Her friends joked that she was so invested in my education that it seemed like she was in school and had graduated with me. She encouraged my writing long before

I ever published a single word. Granny taught me compassion and how to care for others—whether I birthed them or not; whether they are related to me by blood or not. Her mothering prepared me to mother her when she developed Alzheimer's disease. This is my motherhood legacy.

I will never be a mother. But I will always be my grandmother's child.

9

I'm Not a Slut in the Street

I.

A Black woman's primary objective when obtaining medical care is to avoid being treated like a slut in the street. Sluts are girls and women whom others believe to be sexually promiscuous. Society shames sluts and treats them as if they are unworthy of care or concern. People do not believe sluts when they complain. Sluts are viewed as existing only for the pleasure and purpose of men. Every Black woman and girl is always at risk of being treated like a slut in the street, whether we are promiscuous or not. Whether we are sexually active or not. My search for medical care has always involved attempts to avoid being treated like a slut in the street—meaning, my search for medical care has always involved ducking and dodging doctors who are racist, sexist, or just your garden-variety brand of offensive. Unfortunately, I have not always been successful.

In my twenties, I went to a clinic a few blocks from our house to get evaluated for what I believed was polycystic ovary syndrome (PCOS). Based on my Google research, I'd deduced that PCOS might be the cause of my irregular periods that came too frequently, my plentiful chin hairs, and sideburns that rivaled Richard Roundtree's in the movie *Shaft*. The gynecologist, an Asian woman who looked to be as young as me, decided to start with a pelvic exam. There was only one problem: my hymen.

"You're a virgin? Really? You're an attorney?" the doctor kept asking. I don't know if she was more surprised that I was a virgin, that I was an attorney, or that I was an attorney who was also a virgin. Perhaps I differed from her expectations of what young Black women in East New York were like.

"I've only ever conducted an exam on a virgin once," she explained. She probably didn't have many patients who were attorneys, but were virgins really that scarce?

"The patient was Muslim and about to get married. Her family wanted me to examine her before the wedding." I stared at the doctor, wondering why she thought it was morally and professionally permissible to conduct virginity tests. I thought about the patient—how old she was; whether her parents had been in the room during her exam; whether the doctor concluded she was a virgin; and what would've happened had the doctor concluded she wasn't. I wondered what she was thinking during the exam. Did the exam feel cold, transactional, and impersonal? Did she share my terrorizing dread at the mere thought of GYN visits? Did she even want to get married?

Unless I was Muslim and about to be betrothed to a man in waiting, the doctor was unwilling to rattle her nerves for the sake of my reproductive health. It was just as well. She probably tortured and traumatized that young woman.

Although the doctor refused to examine me, she at least referred me to an endocrinologist at a nearby hospital after my blood test results showed that certain hormone levels were higher than normal. She also sent me friend requests on social media. She couldn't tell me what my cervix looked like, but at least she thought I'd make a good buddy.

I was relieved to learn that the endocrinologist my gynecologist had referred me to was the chairman of his department. I thought this meant I'd be treated by the best, by a doctor who had years of experience and would finally be able to give me some answers. However, I was quickly disabused of my optimism. I told him about the symptoms that made me believe I had PCOS: irregular periods and excessive body hair. He asked me some background questions, took my blood pressure, and weighed me.

"Have you always been this heavy?" he asked as he moved the weights on the scale. *You mean, "Have I always been fat?"* First of all, his question was offensive. Second of all, I wasn't "heavy" or fat. I wasn't skinny, but I wasn't heavy either. Although I fell into the "overweight" category of whatever BMI chart he was using, these charts weren't created with Black folks as the standard body type. I couldn't remember a time when I'd ever been considered thin, even when I wore a size six and you could see my clavicles. I'd always had plenty of hips and thighs.

"Are you dating?" he asked.

"Yes." Although I wasn't ready to regale him with my numerous eHarmony stories, I thought this might lead into a discussion about him prescribing me birth control pills—a common way to regulate hormones for patients with PCOS.

"Do you date Jamaican men?"

"What?"

"You mentioned your body hair," he explained. "Jamaican men don't mind their women having a lot of body hair." So now this elderly, white man was an expert on the mating practices of Jamaican men. Okay.

I didn't answer.

His comment was laden with all kinds of assumptions and stereotypes: that I was straight; that I was sexually active; that my medical treatment should be dictated by his racist notions and men's preferences. I suppose that if dating Jamaican men didn't work, he'd try a more aggressive course of treatment for my PCOS.

The doctor did not prescribe me any birth control pills that day. And I did not change my dating site profiles to include the tagline, "Furry Lady in Search of Jamaican Studmuffin." Instead, I left his office with a photocopied low-carb diet plan and a vow to stay as far away from doctors as possible.

II.

After numerous tests, the emergency room physician told me Granny had vascular dementia. We'd ended up in the ER because Granny called the police on the invisible people, and then the police called the ambulance on Granny.

I recounted Granny's hallucinations to her primary care physician during a follow-up appointment. "She yells at the parents for leaving their kids at our house."

"What did she do for a living before she retired?" her doctor asked me.

"She was a foster parent and also babysat children while their parents were at work."

"That explains her hallucinations involving children. Patients who hallucinate, especially the elderly, often have hallucinations involving elements of their past," she explained.

"The doctor in the emergency room told me Granny had a series of ministrokes, which caused her vascular dementia."

"Hmmmm, but the ministrokes don't account for her psychotic symptoms," she said, more to herself than to me.

All the while, Granny sat silently in her chair across from us, her lips pressed tightly together and poked out. She looked straight ahead, refusing to look at either of us. The doctor whispered as she spoke to me and I followed suit, as if whatever ailment was causing Granny's memory loss and hallucinations had also erased her ability to hear and understand English. I stared at the doctor and hoped my eyes telepathically conveyed the message, *You know she can hear us, right?* Granted, there's never a diplomatic way to talk about someone's hallucinations when they're sitting in front of you believing their hallucinations are real. But I couldn't leave Granny in the waiting room while I spoke to the doctor, because she might run off and get lost. In hindsight, we could've included Granny in the conversation or found a way to talk about her symptoms that didn't make her feel excluded or like she was making up stories. I was so desperate to get Granny help that all common sense went out the window.

After the doctor and I talked for a few more minutes, Granny suddenly got up and stormed out of the office, out of the clinic, and into the street without her cane. I ran after her, catching up to her as she was about to jaywalk across a six-lane street. She was headed in the opposite direction of home.

"Granny, wait! Where are you going?"

"I'm not going back in there. I'm not a slut in the street and I am not crazy or senile," she answered.

"Okay. You don't have to stay anywhere you don't want to. But come back inside with me so we can get our things," I tried to reason with her. When we returned to her doctor's office, Granny stood at the door as I apologized to the doctor and collected our bags and Granny's cane. Ice cream always cheered Granny up so we walked to the Wendy's across the street, where we enjoyed chocolate Frostys.

Elderly Black women are not exempt from being treated like sluts in the street. Granny's primary care physician referred her to a neurologist so that the cause of her hallucinations and delusions could be further assessed. She referred us to the neurologist who was treating her mother-in-law for Alzheimer's disease. When we visited him, he prescribed Risperdal to help decrease Granny's psychotic symptoms.

Risperdal was typically used to treat schizophrenia but was also pre-scribed "off-label" to treat psychosis or agitation associated with de-mentia. While it did control the appearance of the invisible people, it also caused a lot of side effects as soon as Granny began taking it. She fell asleep shortly after taking the Risperdal, even while sitting up; it caused her speech to slur; and it made her drool. I was also concerned about the long list of possible serious side effects I'd read on the insert the Pathmark pharmacy had provided, which included:

→ Severe dizziness and fainting. (*Granny was clumsy on a good day.*)

→ Seizures. (*Granny had seizures in the past.*)

→ Risk of death, strokes, and transient ischemic attacks (TIAs or ministrokes) in elderly people with behavior problems due to dementia. (*Granny previously had several ministrokes and was the poster child for "elderly people with behavior problems due to dementia."*)

→ Risk of sudden cardiac death due to an arrhythmia. (*I didn't want to wait around to see if she'd experience sudden death by irregular heartbeat.*)

At Granny's next appointment, I spoke to her neurologist about the side effects and asked whether he could prescribe her another medication.

"My grandmother has had just about every side effect this med-icine can cause," I told him. "The only one left is death."

"Well, how long do you want her to live?" he asked, as if she were a half-dead plant I'd bought at the corner fruit stand. As if her death were not only inevitable, but imminent.

"As long as she can," I answered incredulously.

I wondered why he would ask such a question. Why wasn't it a foregone conclusion that I would want her to live for as long as possible beyond her seventy years? Of course, I would want my grandmother to be unharmed in receiving medical care and to maintain a good quality of life. Why did he assume I would want anything less for my grandmother than he would want for his own mother or grandmother?

When I told Granny's PCP what had happened, she said, "That's surprising. He's never been that way with my family." Of course, he hadn't. It was to be expected that he'd be on his best behavior with a fellow doctor and her loved one, because he would face consequences for treating them poorly. Granny did not have such security. To him, Granny was just another Black woman. Just another medical record number. The potential loss of her life was meaningless to him.

Granny and I did not leave the neurologist's office with a prescription for another type of medication; nor did he provide any insight into how to better manage Risperdal's side effects. I knew we would not be returning. Experience had taught me not to dismiss such behavior by doctors as mere "insensitivity" or poor bedside manner. I needed to find Granny another doctor.

Granny's hallucinations often involved sex, which was surprising given her conservative, religious nature. But it was also a good opportunity to have all the sex talks I could never have with her before she developed Alzheimer's.

"Don't sit in that chair," Granny once yelled at me.

"Why?"

"The pastor's daughter and that boy have oral sex there."

"How do you know they're having oral sex? What were they

doing?" Other than Granny's occasional proclamation that oral sex causes brain cancer, we'd never discussed sex—oral or otherwise.

"They were sucking on each other's privates," Granny replied.

"What do you know about oral sex?"

"I know a whole lot. More than you think I do," she replied. "How do you think you got here?"

The invisibles were having sex everywhere. Buck naked on our front porch. In our backyard. Unbeknownst to me, I was even having sex indiscriminately.

"I haven't seen Jodi in days," Granny told her best friend Sister Christine one day as I sat on the couch reading in the next room, listening to their phone conversation.

"She be upstairs havin' sex with some man." I couldn't remember the last time I'd been on a date.

"I see his britches thrown over the banister," she added. I silently laughed because I hadn't heard anyone use the word britches in years. Besides, there was only a black-and-white tweed coat on the banister, which we used whenever we needed to run outside to open the gate or put the trash out.

"I hear them makin' noises, but I don't say nothin'," she said in a pitiful, weary drawl. Granny could have written erotica in another life.

Worried that Sister Christine might think I had abandoned Granny for a days-long orgy, I walked into her room while she was still on the telephone.

"When did you come in?" Granny asked with surprise.

"I've been here all along. I was sitting on the couch."

"Oh! Girl, don't scare me like that again."

When we'd visited the Brooklyn Memory Clinic several years prior, I described Granny's sex-filled hallucinations to the psychiatrist conducting Granny's assessment.

"Was she ever sexually abused or assaulted?" he asked me.

"Her stepfather molested her when she was a child," I replied.

"That would explain why her hallucinations often involve sex," he said. "It's her brain's way of processing that trauma."

Granny didn't have access to therapists as a child. Nor were they part of her lexicon as an adult. She sought community with other sexual abuse survivors by watching *The Oprah Winfrey Show*, finding a kindred spirit whenever Oprah or her guests talked about their own experiences of sexual abuse.

The sexual abuse Granny endured influenced more than her hallucinations. Her obsession with not being perceived as "a slut in the street" was rooted in that abuse and her lifelong fear of not being believed.

Liar. Crazy. Attention seeker. Those were the typical responses from family members whenever Granny talked about being sexually abused by her stepfather. They said it with their silence and dismissive looks. Those there-she-goes-again glances at one another. I was too young to ask why they thought she would make something like that up, or why it was unimaginable that a man would molest his stepchild or biological child. It's not as if it's uncommon or unheard of for such a thing to happen. Shortly after Granny's death, a family member told me, "Your grandmother made that up. That was all in her head." *But you weren't there and didn't even know Granny when she was a child*, I thought. But I didn't respond. I didn't need to convince anyone, nor did I need convincing. I had always believed Granny. Perhaps she had been called a liar as a twelve-year-old girl, or was told that she was "fast" or promiscuous. Maybe she'd even been called a slut. Black girls are often called "fast" for a variety of reasons: for crossing our legs when we're seated; when our hips and breasts seem wide beyond our years; when adult men leer at us as we pass by; and when we accuse men of stealing our innocence. Black girls are shamed for merely existing in our skin. Granny had spent most of her life not being believed. To her, being a liar and a slut in the street were the worst things a Black girl or woman could be.

III.

"You know you gon have to fight, right?" my friend Safiya asked when I told her I'd been diagnosed with breast cancer.

"Yup, I know."

Her statement did not need an explanation. Any Black person understood exactly what she meant. When she said I would have to fight, she didn't mean "fight" as in "hold on to my will to live," or "fight cancer with all the courage and resilience I could muster." Nor did she mean I would need to fight against the side effects of my medical treatment. She meant that I'd have to fight to receive competent care because medical professionals routinely ignore Black people's complaints and provide us with subpar treatment. Studies show that doctors and nurses are less likely to believe Black patients when we say we're in pain, and they treat our pain less aggressively than they do white patients'—if they treat it at all. We experience worse health outcomes than our white counterparts, even when our education and incomes are the same. Safiya and I could run down a laundry list of all the times doctors had ignored, dismissed, or misdiagnosed our symptoms. We could pinpoint those times when doctors weren't aggressive or thorough in our treatment and we wondered whether they'd provided our white counterparts with the same quality of care.

I went down the rabbit hole of research about health disparities for Black women with breast cancer. Black women have the lowest five-year survival rate for every stage of diagnosis and subtype of breast cancer.[*] Although we have a 4 percent lower incidence rate of breast cancer than white women, we're 40 percent more likely to die from the disease.[†] The death rate for Black women younger than age 50 is twice as high as the death rate for white women in that age group.[‡] I read about factors that commonly affect Black women's survival rates: early detection; access to and type of health insurance; access to screening and care; how quickly treatment starts after diagnosis; our ability to take time off work and get assistance with household responsibilities. The list went on and on. Safiya was right. I would have to fight.

The Black Patient's Guide to Avoid Being Treated Like a Slut in the Street[*]

These rules are meant to make you appear worthy of receiving competent medical care and increase the likelihood that your complaints will be believed. When you attend medical appointments, you should do the following:

1. Speak proper English, not Ebonics or African American Vernacular English (AAVE). It'll make you sound educated.

2. Dress like you're going to work in an office.

3. Mention that you went to college. If you went to graduate school, throw that in for good measure. If you didn't attend college, see Rule #1.

---

[*] Sandy McDowell, "Breast Cancer Death Rates Are Highest for Black Women—Again," American Cancer Society, October 3, 2022. Accessed March 29, 2023. https://www.cancer.org/latest-news/breast-cancer-death-rates-are-highest-for-black-women-again.html.

[†] Ibid.

[‡] Ibid.

4. If you are a physician or attorney, or married to one, mention that.

5. Do a lot of research so you can ask questions that are so thoughtful and detailed that your doctors will ask if you went to medical school.

6. Perfect your official, professional "I am very concerned" voice for when things go wrong. You must carefully modulate your voice so that you don't give off "angry Black person" vibes.

7. When researching doctors online, look for the Black patients' reviews.

8. Get doctor recommendations from other Black folks.

9. When your body doesn't feel right or something seems wrong, keep calling everybody and their momma until someone listens to you. Have your doctor's office on speed dial so often that they won't even have to ask, "Who is it?" when you call.

10. If you can, take someone with you who can follow these rules. If not, make sure your emergency contact is updated and that other folks know about your medical care.

11. When all else fails, switch doctors.

* *This guidance does not constitute medical advice or establish a doctor-patient relationship. We cannot guarantee your health outcomes. One can never tell with these things, and you are still Black in a world full of systemic discrimination. In case of emergencies, please call 911 and seek medical attention. Stay woke.*

IV.

I was in elementary school the first time I had suicidal ideations. I didn't feel anyone liked me, I was being bullied at school, and Granny was always fussing at me about one thing or another. I was also being sexually abused by a neighbor. To block people out, I'd pretend not to hear them when they asked me something. "You didn't hear me talking to you? We need to get your ears checked," Granny would tell me. I tried to kill myself by taking a bunch of Granny's pills she kept on top of the refrigerator. Imagine my surprise when I found myself still alive. Granny never realized I'd taken her pills.

My junior year of high school Granny fell face-first on Pitkin Avenue. It was never clear whether she'd tripped on something or simply lost her balance, but she hit her head so hard that my neighbor heard the impact up the street and looked back to see what happened. After someone called 911, my neighbor ran around the corner to my house.

"Your grandmother fell," he told me, out of breath. We ran back to Granny and I rode in the ambulance with her to St. Mary's Hospital.

"I'm okay," she told me as I stood beside her bed in the ER and cried. But she didn't look okay. Her face was scraped up and her mouth was bloody. Several of her bottom teeth were damaged during the fall and eventually had to be extracted. One of her front top teeth shifted forward, and two of them chipped. After her fall, Granny sometimes tried to hide her crooked smile in pictures by stiffly keeping her top lip over her upper row of teeth. "Smile normally," I would tell her. Granny was a pretty lady, crooked smile and all.

A Black nurse came over to obtain information about Granny.

"Is your grandmother on any antipsychotic medications?" she asked.

"No. She's not crazy," I replied through tears. I became so distraught that the nurse apologized to me.

"I didn't mean to offend you."

After numerous tests, doctors determined that Granny fell because she had suffered a seizure. They prescribed Depakote to control her seizures; this medication was also used to treat bipolar disorder. The seizures left her so incapacitated that she was assigned a home attendant and began receiving Supplemental Security Income (SSI) benefits, for which I became her representative payee while still in high school. Now, almost twenty-five years later, the nurse's question doesn't seem offensive at all. Asking if she was taking any antipsychotic medications seems perfectly reasonable when considering whether to prescribe a medication that is used to treat seizures and bipolar disorder. At the time, however, I feared that doctors wouldn't take her pain seriously if they thought she had a mental illness. I was afraid they wouldn't believe her.

I was depressed my sophomore year at Barnard. I stayed in bed for days and cried all the time. I had a group of friends and participated in school activities, and yet I felt as if I didn't belong anywhere. My roommate gave me silent, worried looks. *I should've gone to NYU*, I thought. I really thought my school choice was the cause of my unhappiness. But I'd completed my first year at Barnard and loved it. Granny sensed something was wrong and took a cab from Brooklyn to my dorm at 116th Street in the city. When she walked into my room, my roommate left and stayed gone for the rest of the day. As I lay in bed crying, Granny sat beside me in a chair and prayed and wrote in the spirit in the notebook she'd brought with her. We never spoke about why I was sad. She kept watch and didn't leave until nighttime. A few days later she ordered me a TV/VCR combo from Fingerhut and gave me money so I could have the cable turned on in my dorm room. I was depressed but we didn't have a name for what ailed me. Prayer and a TV were the only medicines Granny knew.

The emergency room doctors diagnosed Granny with vascular dementia, gave her a two-week supply of Seroquel to quell her hallucinations, and sent us on our way. I asked Granny's primary care physician for a refill at Granny's next appointment.

"I don't feel comfortable prescribing antipsychotic medication," her doctor told me. I panicked because it took forever to get appointments when you had Medicaid and Medicare, and I was afraid we'd run out of medication. Granny's doctor referred her to a mental health clinic at Jamaica Hospital. Granny would need to be assessed by a therapist and psychiatrist before being given a new prescription. As we were leaving her therapy appointment, the therapist informed Granny of the next phase of her evaluation.

"You'll need to come back in two weeks to be evaluated by the psychiatrist," the therapist told my stern-looking Granny.

"No, I'm not coming back," Granny replied.

"Why not?"

"I'm not senile. I don't see nobody named Nile."

"He's just going to evaluate you to see how we can help you," the therapist continued.

"If I agree to see a psychiatrist, then I'd be admitting that something is wrong with me," Granny explained in a matter-of-fact manner. Granny's wild hallucinations, which included funerals in her closet and folks defecating in our backyard, demonstrated that something was very wrong with her. The therapist and I exchanged looks that said, *Yeah, she does have a point.*

"Ms. McKinney, here's your clinic card with your next appointment date and time on it," the therapist responded with a defeated look on her face. We never returned to the clinic.

V.

Grief over Granny's death snuck up on me at the most inopportune times. I cried all the time and everywhere—home, work, during my commutes, in the middle of conversations unrelated to Granny. When I started crying on my way home from work, I got off the train and went to the movies so I could cry in the dark without anyone noticing. One night while sitting at my desk in my bedroom, I pleaded with an invisible Granny, "Whyyyyyyyyy did you have to leave me? You know I need you!" I cried until I gave myself a headache. *How could God take away the most important person to me? How dare God do this to me!* And then I abruptly stopped crying and laughed as I imagined Granny furiously shaking her head and saying very harshly, "Stop it! Stop making all that noise." Granny was not a fan of dramatic displays of emotion. The next day at work, a colleague saw my puffy eyes and asked if I was okay. "Yup. I just need to take some Claritin for my allergies," I told her.

Grief is a stealthy culprit that constantly changes shapes. It comes in the form of headache-inducing tears. It is the sometimes pounding, other times subtle, but ever-present heaviness that bears down on your chest and hampers your breathing. It makes your heart race and skip beats. Grief is a veil that floats through the air, wrapping mundane acts of daily living in memories of your loved one. I saw reminders of Granny everywhere. An elderly woman walking up the subway steps reminded me of my law school days when Granny used to wait for me at that train station every night so I wouldn't have to walk home alone. Every time I bought take-out food, I remembered how I used to bring food home after work and share it with Granny as we watched TV and talked.

When a coworker came to my office and asked how I was doing, I began to cry. She closed the door, walked over to my desk, and hugged me.

"Maybe you should go talk to someone," she said. It was the first time anyone had ever suggested I see a therapist. I knew she was right. I spent my weekends buried under the covers in Granny's bed with the curtains and blinds closed. I wore the same pajama shirt for months, because it still smelled of the sweet and acrid odor of Granny's hospital room. Although it smelled like sickness and death, it reminded me that she was once alive. My friend Samantha called me every day to make sure I was still alive, because I'd told her I no longer wanted to live.

I searched PsychologyToday.com for therapists who specialized in grief therapy and were Black women. I wanted a therapist who'd be able to understand my experiences as a Black woman. I made a list and began calling them that day. Some never returned my call; some didn't have appointments available for several weeks; and others had irregular hours. One of the therapists who called me back was a white woman with a nose ring, tattoos, and a welcoming smile. I'd contacted her because her face in her profile picture looked friendly and comforting. When she called me, her voice was so soothing that I cried and bore my soul. She saw me later that week. Her casual, relaxed style was far different from the formal, glasses-on-the-tip-of-the-nose, legal pad–toting image of therapists I'd had in my head. Not only was she not what I expected a therapist to look like, but I wondered how someone so different from me, a white woman, would be able to understand and help me. For the next few years, I visited her office once a week and we pieced my life back together. We talked about my grief and so many other aspects of my life. I finally stopped to think about what *I* wanted and needed. I began to envision and plan for a future without Granny—a future in which I could be happy. It was also the first time I'd been diagnosed as being depressed. It's been more than ten years since I walked into her Upper West Side office. My therapist saved my life.

Although Granny suffered many losses throughout her life, we never talked about how to cope with loss. It wasn't until the end of her life that I got a glimpse of her grief. Granny eventually began seeing a therapist and psychiatrist once a month. She spent about thirty minutes talking to a therapist, followed by a meeting with her psychiatrist next door to assess her progress on her antipsychotic medication. I always sat in these sessions with Granny. They weren't the traditional "let's see how we can uncover your childhood trauma and life patterns to improve your life" type therapy sessions. Granny talked about whatever was on her mind. Sometimes she complained about me telling her what to do all the time. Other times she complained about the invisible people squatting in our house. If our prior attempts to get her to attend therapy had been accompanied by the caveat, "You'll be able to chat about whatever you want," we could've gotten her to a therapist and psychiatrist years earlier.

During her last therapy session, a month or so before her death, she talked about her grief.

"I just found out a dear friend of mine is very sick," she told her therapist. Her sick friend was "the one who got away." They'd dated many years ago when my mother was a child. Although she had not seen him in many years, she was still friends with his family. They'd informed Granny about his illness.

"So many of my friends are dying," she said as she cried. Her friends were up in age, many of them older or sicker than her. Although she slipped in and out of lucidity most days, she still remembered the finality of death and grief's sorrow. Alzheimer's had not taken that from her.

Several years before that therapy session, Granny and I had gone to the hospital to visit a friend, but by the time we arrived, the friend had passed away. Friends and family stood in a circle around her bed, held hands, and prayed for her safe passage to the afterlife. I wasn't sure Granny understood what was happening. She prayed for our friend, laid hands on her warm body, and wrote in the spirit—just as she'd done many times before when visiting people in the hospital. She ripped out a page of her writing from her book and placed it on our friend's hospital bed, as if it might heal our friend after we left. When Granny looked up at our neighbor lying in her bed with her eyes closed, recognition crept across her face and into her voice.

"She's dead," Granny told me.

"Yes, she is." I ushered her out of the room before her tears began to fall.

When I called Granny's therapist to let him know she had passed away, his voice choked up as he offered his condolences. He ended the call so he could go compose himself. When he called me back a few days later to see how I was doing, I filled him in on Granny's last month in the hospital.

Given my and Granny's experiences with medical professionals, I was surprised that her therapist had been so overcome with emotion. His vulnerability let me know Granny wasn't just a number to him. He had actually listened to her stories and knew how special she was.

The receptionist at Granny's doctors' office had a similar reaction when I told her the news.

"She was such a nice lady," she told me as she cried.

I abruptly got off the phone to stop myself from joining her cry fest.

Granny had started going to that medical office several years prior. One of her home attendants was a regular patient there and had highly recommended the doctors. The medical practice was run by a white father-son duo who dressed like they worked on Wall Street instead of in a medical office. The son, married with young kids, had a quiet demeanor and wore suits. The elderly dad, a loud jokester who serenaded patients with Frank Sinatra songs, wore dress pants with a shirt and tie. Although the dad's office and desk were cluttered with papers, books, and memorabilia, framed pictures of his wife, children, and grandchildren peeked out from among the piles. Their staff, including the receptionist, had worked there for years. Going to that medical office was like going to the fictional bar on the TV show *Cheers*. The staff knew all the patients' names, ailments, and melodramas. No matter what new symptom or complaint Granny had, her doctors always figured out the cause and treatment. And Granny never left their office traumatized or feeling like a slut in the street.

It was one of the few medical offices I'd visited that wasn't affiliated with a hospital or medical system, where you could have your blood drawn and EKGs performed on site, and where you didn't have to wait all day to be seen. It was also one of the few medical offices I'd been to that didn't treat only patients of color and patients who received Medicaid and Medicare, but that also treated white patients and patients with private insurance. The inclusion of white patients and additional funding sources translated to more resources and better care than Granny had received in our majority Black and Hispanic neighborhood.

Because I didn't go to the doctor as often as I should have, I didn't have a primary care physician of my own, so I went to one of Granny's doctors when I became ill several months after she had passed away. When he finished examining me, a tech, who was familiar from my visits with Granny, ushered me to another room to conduct an EKG. Other than me complimenting her on her gray, impeccably styled and well-moisturized twists, we'd never chatted much. She didn't talk much to any of the patients. She simply did her job and kept the traffic steadily flowing into and out of her EKG kingdom. I laid there quietly as she placed the electrodes on my chest. Despite the silence, it was comforting to be back at Granny's old medical stomping ground. Before the tech began my test, she spoke to me.

"We took care of your grandmother. Now, we're going to take care of you."

I smiled and closed my eyes. I was finally in good hands.

10

The Things She Left Behind

I.

I hoard memories. I began to hoard the remnants of our lives, the memories and old wounds infused in our DNA, after Granny began losing them. It began out of necessity. Granny was obsessed with toilet tissue, napkins, and paper towels. She placed them everywhere—under her pillows, in every pocket of every coat she owned, in drawers, and purses. Paper helped Granny fulfill her daily mission: to hide things from the invisible people only she could see. She used it to cover items she didn't want the invisible people getting their paws on. The only problem is that she would forget where she hid the items, accuse the invisible people of stealing from her, and then yell at them about how they needed to pay her rent or get out of her house. I felt sorry for the invisible people; they just couldn't catch a break. Not to mention that the piles of tissue, and the things wrapped in them, would inevitably get tossed in the trash. I'm convinced that her missing eyeglasses, dentures, and the ten dollar bill a home attendant gave her for her birthday are now resting in a shroud of two-ply Marcal toilet tissue in a Staten Island landfill. Another downside to Granny's paper obsession is that I could never find any when I needed it. So, I started hiding paper goods in my bedroom, which I kept locked when I wasn't home.

My bedroom became a holding cell for anything I needed to hide from Granny. Plastic bags were the next items to follow. As she did with tissue, Granny placed her belongings in plastic bags so the invisible people wouldn't steal them. It was a hassle to search through every plastic bag in the house whenever I needed something of Granny's, like shoes or a wig or those peach-colored sponge bra inserts she loved to wear. I also grew tired of never having enough bags when trash day rolled around. So, I started keeping the garbage bags in my bedroom as well.

Our house was always well-lit and full of activity at night. Granny experienced sundown syndrome, a common phenomenon among people with Alzheimer's disease and other types of dementia in which patients get confused and agitated as the sun goes down. These symptoms sometimes last through the night. As a result, they don't sleep well and are likely to wander. Granny developed irregular sleeping habits and began losing her sense of time. During the daytime, she'd think it was late at night.

"When are you coming home? It's too late for you to be out," she'd often tell me when I called her from work during the day.

As a result of her dysfunctional internal clock, she got into the most mischief in the middle of the night. She roamed the house like a little ghost, looking for things to get into. She emptied everything out of her closet onto her bed and repeatedly folded and unfolded her clothes with no clear purpose. She also packed and unpacked them into her purses and plastic bags. Embracing her inner supermodel, she sometimes tried on all her clothes before packing them.

"I have to go to work in the morning. If you do not get in bed and go to sleep, I am going upstairs to my room," I'd tell her, slowly emphasizing each word. Sometimes she would oblige me, because she had grown accustomed to me sleeping in her room and didn't want to sleep alone. Most times, however, she would look at me with a bewildered expression on her face.

"What?" she'd ask me, as if it were perfectly normal to organize her clothes at two o'clock in the morning. And then she would continue her packing and unpacking, folding and unfolding, sorting and unsorting—mixed in with admonitions to the invisible people to stop bothering her stuff. On those nights when she ignored me, I'd sometimes retreat to my bedroom upstairs, desperate for sleep even at the risk of her calling 911 on the invisible people or chasing them onto the porch. At other times, I'd angrily turn and face the wall and disappear under the covers to block out the light from her lamp and the noise of her shuffling and rambling.

Granny also developed an obsession with doing laundry and washed clothes in the bathtub during her middle-of-the-night wanderings. She'd soak them in the yellow baby bathtub she bathed me in as an infant and then hang them on the collapsible wooden clothes drying rack in the kitchen. She sometimes placed wet clothes in the washing machine. Since she didn't remember how to work it, the clothes would stay there undetected until I discovered their damp, molded remains and an empty laundry detergent bottle on laundry day. I moved the laundry detergent to my bedroom, putting an end to Granny's daily clothes washing sessions. At ten dollars a pop, hiding the detergent was cheaper and safer for our clothes.

Granny didn't involve me in her nighttime shenanigans unless she really got herself in a bind, like the time I awoke to her poking me as I lay on the couch. I looked up to see her face covered in a dried, white, pasty substance.

"What did you get yourself into? What's that on your face?" I asked her.

"I don't know."

I took Granny's hand and led her to the kitchen sink, where I tried unsuccessfully to rinse the unknown substance off with my hands. I then used a washcloth lathered with soap and hot water to wipe the substance off, still to no avail. Finally, I had to scrub Granny's skin to remove the caked-on substance. She began to cry, frustrated at being scrubbed in the middle of the night when she'd rather be sleeping or sorting clothes. The scene reminded me of how she used to make me sit on the side of our green tub and scrub my knees and elbows with Ajax to get rid of the darkness. She stood watch in the doorway as I cried and scrubbed, but skin and blood were the only things that came off. The blackness remained.

"I'm sorry," I said.

After sudsing and rubbing and scrubbing the paste-like gook off Granny's slippery face, I helped her back to bed and searched every nook and cranny of the bathroom for the mystery substance. I examined every tube and bottle of lotion, soap, deodorant, Polident denture cream, shampoo and conditioner, toothpaste, and cleanser. But nothing looked disturbed or similar in texture to Granny's concoction. I took the safe route and removed everything except soap, toothpaste, and a roll of toilet tissue. I had to buy more plastic storage bins from Target so I could organize the growing pile of contraband in my bedroom.

As Granny's Alzheimer's progressed, I began hiding things that made her anxious or sad. Granny's wigs also went to the holding cell. She used to keep her wigs on top of vases, plastic bottles, and Pringles potato chip containers.

"Those people keep looking at me and won't leave," she often told me while pointing to the makeshift wig mannequins. Sometimes she fussed at the wig people so bad I was worried she'd give herself a stroke. I couldn't have the wigs terrorizing Granny, so I removed them and my bedroom became wig heaven. In her dresser drawer, I left one wig, which she was too vain to lose.

I found a framed photo buried between clothes in one of her drawers. It was a black-and-white picture of her stepfather sitting on a bench with one leg crossed over the other.

"Why is this picture here?"

"That man was mean to me," she answered softly. I always wondered why she'd kept his picture on her dresser with pictures of her mother and other family members for all those years. Had it been me, I would've buried or burned his picture years ago.

As Granny's memory continued to fade, I started hoarding items that represented her lost memories; our family's memories; and memories I never knew existed but had shaped me.

I was at work one day when I got a call from Granny's home attendant Robin.

"Did you mean to throw out a large plastic bag?" she asked.

"I didn't throw anything out today."

"When I took the trash out, I saw a large black plastic bag that wasn't in the can before. I opened it and there were a bunch of papers and pictures inside," Robin replied. I had no idea what bag she was talking about, but we both agreed that Granny must have thrown it out.

"Okay. Just take the bag inside and hide it from Granny. I'll look at it when I get home."

The nondescript plastic bag turned out to be a collection of memories and clues about our past. That night, I hung my mouth open in awe as I examined the treasures Granny had so unceremoniously dumped into the trash.

I laughed as I read a letter Granny's twin brother, my Uncle Bill, had written to her more than fifty years ago, in which he lamented, "I don't have too much to say, because I have so many problems I can't think straight." The bag contained a picture of Granny and Uncle Bill when they were ten years old. Although Uncle Bill looked different, Granny's face hadn't changed much over the years. As I looked at the stern-faced little girl in the black-and-white photo with a ribbon tied on top of her head, I wondered what she was thinking and feeling.

I wondered what her life was like and how she had grown into the woman who would become my grandmother.

I found documents that helped me know Granny and my mother better. Granny's small turquoise diary from 1969, with the lock on the front cover, revealed that she had bestowed me with her writer's spirit. She wrote in her diary every day, in small cursive on a single page. Like me, she was a chronicler of life. She recorded what time she awoke and went to bed; the chores she performed and errands she ran; the groceries she bought and the food she cooked; her job searches and interviews; her dreams and the things that haunted her; family squabbles; major family events like deaths and illnesses; her fears, anxieties, and disappointments. She noted the scriptures she read and the churches at which she preached. In recounting her day's activities, she often wrote that she "did some writing for God" or "wrote in my book." I assume this is what she later referred to as "writing in the spirit," her way of receiving and interpreting God's messages. Writing was how she communicated with God. Someone recently asked me when I feel closest to God. Like Granny, I feel closest to God when I am writing.

I read letters my mother had written to Granny when she was a child, after she'd given birth to me, and while in jail. It was the first time I saw my mother as someone other than a woman who had chosen drugs and her own whims over being a mother and daughter. I also found the guardianship papers Granny obtained from Surrogate's Court when she became my legal guardian. Although Granny had raised me since bringing me home from the hospital after I was born, those papers memorialized the day I officially became Granny's baby.

My mother never had much contact with her father, and Granny didn't offer any details about her own relationship with him other than "I used to pass out during sex." It wasn't until Granny's homegoing that I learned how they'd met. During her remarks, my grandfather's sister told the attendees her family had met Granny while she was taking care of one of their family members, presumably as a home attendant. When I went through Granny's memory bag, I found clues about the nature of their relationship. I discovered criminal court disposition papers regarding my mother's father. Apparently, Granny had filed a police report against him when my mother was a baby. I also saw pay stubs belonging to my grandfather, which Granny had probably kept so she could get a court order for him to pay child support. Years earlier, while my mother was in a residential drug rehab program, she told me that she wrote a letter to her deceased father about the pain of his not being in her life. She also wrote that she forgave him. As a sign of closure and letting go, she burned the letter. Judging by the contents of Granny's bag, perhaps my grandfather's absence had been for the best.

Granny's memory bag also contained many pictures of family members I had known and others who died before I was born. They made me miss Granny's sisters, my Aunt Jennye and Aunt Lil, who died while I was in high school and college.

"Who's this?" I asked Granny while holding out a picture of Aunt Lil as a young woman. Aunt Lil was light-skinned and heavy-set with fat cheeks and curly hair.

She stared at the picture.

"I don't know. That's you," She answered.

I had never seen these items in the thirty-one years I had lived in that house. I wondered where Granny had hidden this bag all those years and how she'd remembered where it was. Examining the contents of Granny's memory bag was like getting to know her for the first time, getting the answers to questions I never thought to ask, coming up with new questions she'd never be able to answer. These items were a link to Granny and our family legacy. I thanked Robin for calling to tell me about the bag. Had Alzheimer's not robbed us, Granny would never have thrown out her memories, our past. I hugged Granny and took her memory bag to my room. It deserved its own sacred plastic bin.

Finding Granny's memory bag was the beginning of my obsession with preserving ephemera and personal archives. Letters, old checks, diaries, mailed envelopes, lists, notes jotted down in old notebooks or on napkins stuck between the pages of Granny's Bibles. Each of these things helped me hold on to Granny; they helped me preserve her memory. These items filled the silences that had endured over generations in my family and helped me map out new stories about the ancestors I loved and the ones I never knew.

II.

I now understand people who leave the bedrooms of their dearly departed just as they were before their loved ones passed away. I used to think these people were stuck in the past and that something was wrong with them. What is normal? And who gets to be the judge, jury, and therapist? Loss changed me. My grief kept me frozen in time. Three months after Granny's death, her bedroom remained unchanged. The clothes she wore to the hospital were still balled up in the plastic bag an ER nurse gave me. Her two packs of Oreo cookies remained in her nightstand drawers. I left her half-eaten croissant in its plastic wrapping in the refrigerator, along with her jar of duck sauce and the prune juice she drank daily to keep her regular. "You need to throw that stuff away. It's not as if she's coming back to eat it," a family member told me. Granny's dirty laundry was still unsorted in her hamper, littered with food stains and still smelling like a mixture of her body musk and the Dior Addict 2 body lotion she loved.

I am one of the mourners of the hoarding variety. Keeping your loved ones' belongings close is also a way of mourning. There is comfort in the familiar. Keeping things just as they were is an attempt to freeze time. Yes, you know your loved one is gone and will never return. Yes, you have all your memories of them. No, you can't keep things as they were forever or bring your loved one back. But just for a little while longer, you want to feel their presence. Just for a little while longer, you want to savor the images of their happy, healthy, living selves.

III.

Although the television show *Hoarders* popularized the term, I had never heard of *hoarding* while growing up. We didn't refer to people as hoarders, even when they fit the definition. The first obvious hoarder I knew was Mr. Maxwell, an elderly white man who lived across the street from us when I was a little girl. His living room was full of unplugged televisions. His house number was written in white paint on each one. I don't know if they even worked.

Granny was the first undercover hoarder I knew. She was a neat freak and cleaning fanatic. She was so committed to orderliness that, when her twin brother lived with her when they were young adults, Granny used to put signs on the couch that said, "Please do not sit here." She always said God required that everything be "in decency and in order," and that "cleanliness is next to godliness." However, she was also a packrat. She never threw anything away. There was never spring cleaning in our house, only organized ways to store all our things. Everything had a place. Consequently, I never threw things away either. I never discarded or donated clothes. If I no longer wore them, I simply kept them until they disappeared.

Paper was a special kind of evil. We kept old bills, store catalogs, and flyers, my FAFSA applications for college, old tax returns, homework assignments, and other randomness. I still have a suitcase full of Granny's old bank statements, canceled checks, and bills from the 1970s. Some of the banks and utility companies went out of business decades ago. Why did Granny keep these things and why am I still holding on to them? There is no reason for me to still have my home-work assignments from the first grade. But here we are.

I panicked when I saw the email from the storage facility. Their land-lord hadn't renewed their lease, they were closing, and I had thirty days to clear my stuff out. I hadn't been to my storage unit since the day I dropped off all my boxes, plastic storage bins, suitcases, and vac-uum cleaner eight years ago.

The storage unit contained items I'd brought with me when I sold our house. Most of the things were Granny's. At least I'd had enough forethought to label the boxes, which would help when I eventually went through them: "Granny's Clothes and Purses," "Granny's Dress Clothes," "Granny's and Jodi's Papers," "Granny's Clothes." These were things I could not part with, even after numerous rounds of purging.

Prior to moving, I tried getting rid of things in stages. First, I took pictures of some of her suits and purses, with plans to donate them afterwards. But I started crying and put everything back in her closet. I gave some of Granny's belongings to her friends. One of her home attendants asked for a purse I'd bought Granny during my trip to Paris. *This purse is not Granny. Granny is not this purse,* I repeated to convince myself to let the purse go. It was a coping technique I'd read about in some self-help article or book.

There's nothing like a deadline to light a fire under you. When we finally had a closing date to sell the house, my purging efforts went into high gear. I stuffed some of Granny's coats and clothes into my red shopping cart and pushed them to the Spanish-speaking Pente-costal church around the corner from our house. I donated other things to Housing Works, a nonprofit that operates thrift stores. I only threw out the more impersonal things, like furniture that I couldn't take with me to my new apartment. I brought everything else with me. These were things I couldn't bring myself to throw or give away.

Storage units are not cheap. I've spent so much money holding on to things—boxes whose contents I can't even remember. *But what if there's something important in there*, I tell myself.

I moved all of Granny's things to another storage facility nearby.

I know how you become a hoarder. Through sadness. Through grief. You lose something or someone and you slide further down the hole and you lose hope and you become overwhelmed and you just stop trying. And one day you wake up surrounded by your stuff. You don't even remember how or when it got so bad.

Granny has more closet space than me in my apartment. Her clothes are so intermingled with mine that a stranger might think she lives with me. I never realized how much of Granny's stuff I had and how out of control it was until I saw my apartment through the eyes of others.

I had a bunch of boxes in my living room when a maintenance guy came to fix my leaking ceiling. He asked, "What happened?" when he saw them. I pretended not to hear him.

"Are you moving?" another guy asked when he came to pick up the items I wanted to place in storage.

"No." I was too embarrassed to tell him I'd been living there for over a year.

When I broke my ankle a few years ago, a friend came over and helped me declutter so I could maneuver around my apartment. I sat on the couch, resigned as she threw out multiple items in the boxes and piles on my living room floor. There really was no use for the broken white colander trimmed in blue. Granny used it whenever she made mac and cheese. I would never again use the reading pillow I'd had since my first year of college, whose stitching Granny had resewn several times before coming undone again.

"You should see a therapist to address the grief of losing your grandmother," she said as she dumped items into a garbage bag. I was too embarrassed to tell her that I'd already been to therapy and that I had stopped after a few years because I thought I was "taking too long" to grieve. When I eventually returned to therapy, I wasn't honest with my therapist about the extent of my hoarding.

I hadn't realized how obvious my grief was. I thought I'd done a good job of hiding it, a good job of showing the world that I had it all together. But my grief was so palpable and all-consuming that I wore it like clothing. My sadness and Granny's things were all around me and were my security blanket.

When you keep so many unnecessary items, you can never locate and properly preserve the important things. The good stuff is hiding underneath all those receipts, magazines, and canceled checks. The author Jason Reynolds preserves the memories and mementos of his loved ones who've passed away by making them part of his home decor. His grandfather's last pack of cigarettes, Pall Mall Gold 100s, and their accompanying book of matches are mounted in a gold-colored frame.* A long, rectangular-shaped brown frame containing the contents of his grandmother's wallet—including her voter registration card and her first application for a government job—hangs in the entryway of his home.† By showcasing these items, Reynolds keeps them and his loved ones close, while also illuminating their significance. I would love to honor Granny and the things she left behind in a similar way.

The problem with having so much stuff is that it weighs you

---

* Erika Gonzalez, "Author Jason Reynolds Opens the Doors to His New DC Home," *4 Your Home*, NBC 4 Washington. Accessed March 30, 2023. https://www.nbcwashington.com/news/local/dc-area-real-estate/author-jason-reynolds-opens-the-doors-to-his-new-dc-home/2772767/.

† "The Story of Jason Reynolds' Cool and Creative Row Home," *HGTV Magazine*, August 12, 2020. https://www.hgtv.com/design/home-tours/tour-jason-reynolds-washington-dc-home-pictures.

down. I imagine what it might feel like to have closets full of my own things, what it might feel like to spread out. I follow Instagram accounts of clutter-free spaces for inspiration. #Studygram accounts. Interior design, home décor, and home organization influencers.

I've heard plenty of stories about people who've lost everything they owned in floods, fires, hurricanes, and other natural disasters. If I had to pack in a hurry and could only take the most important things with me, I wouldn't know what to grab first. Maybe that's a good place to start.

Emergency Evacuation List

1. Her diary and letters
2. Her birth certificate
3. One of her Bibles
4. The copy of *Acts of Faith* by Iyanla Vanzant that I gave her for Mother's Day in 1992
5. The pressed, salt-and-pepper lock of her hair the funeral director gave me
6. Her fifth-grade picture and report card
7. The picture we took that day in the picture booth at Kings Plaza Mall
8. Cassette tapes of her voice
9. Her phonebook
10. Her pink blanket I covered her with every night
11. One of her favorite sweaters
12. One of her tiaras
13. The multicolored housedress Aunt Chris gave her years ago
14. A couple of her church suits
15. Her hat box and at least one of her church hats

I periodically check my various boxes, bags, suitcases, drawers, and closets to make sure I still have the things on this list. In moments of panic, I get up in the middle of the night to search for an item that has crossed my mind. Sometimes my search lasts a few minutes, sometimes I don't finish until hours later when night has turned to day.

I used to make New Year's resolutions every year, but I usually didn't achieve them and ended up in the same place or worse off a year later. Then I started a more helpful annual goal-setting ritual: I come up with a different theme each year to guide my intentions and efforts. This year, my themes are "order" and "joy." I need more of both in my life. Maybe this is the year I'll tackle all the things and memories that have kept me stuck. Maybe I'll finally loosen my grip on the past and find more joy in the present. Maybe this will be the year I fill my life with newness: new memories, new people, new space, new air, new love, new joy. Granny's things are not Granny. As long as I've got my stories and memories, she'll never die. Love never dies.

11

Some Useful Advice for Going to Meet Your Dead Loved One and Other Tragedies

I have never been more aware of my singleness than when Granny was dying. I was standing in her hospital room as one of her doctors gave me the reality check I'd been avoiding.

"We'll continue treating her because we have to, but there's nothing else we can do," the doctor told me. Although several doctors were present, she was the only one who spoke to me—the only one whose face I saw in the dim room. She must have been the designated bearer of bad news and the others were just there for moral support or observation. She had called me several weeks earlier to inform me that Granny had taken a turn for the worse.

"Your grandmother had problems breathing, was turning blue, and not getting enough oxygen, so we had to intubate her," she'd said as I anxiously interrupted with an "Okay????" after every few words, hoping that what followed wouldn't be any worse than what she'd already said.

Since our initial phone call, Granny's prognosis had changed from unknown to critical to cautiously optimistic to dying.

"Do you have a husband?" the doctor asked me.

"No."

"A boyfriend?"

"No."

"Ohhhh," she said in that sorrowful, drawn-out way echoed by those who pity women past thirty who are still unmarried and childless with nary a prospect of either in sight.

My grandmother was dying and the only thing this nosy woman cared about was whether I had a man stashed somewhere. "Is there anyone who can come be with you?" she added.

"No."

That's when it dawned on me that the doctor wasn't trying to shame me for being unmarried. Instead, she wanted to ensure I had the appropriate support as I faced Granny's death. *I've done everything else by myself up to this point. Why would I need someone here with me now?* I'd thought. It was the ignorance and indignation of the uninitiated. If you've never lost someone close to you, or watched a loved one die, you might underestimate the need for support from others. I had been so used to caring for Granny on my own that I never imagined needing someone else to help me as she neared death. Throughout Granny's Alzheimer's journey, it had always been just the two of us. Home attendants and friends guest starred in our show, but our family was in Florida and I was with her every day. Me and Granny: the two sister girls. Despite working full time, I took Granny to every doctor's appointment. I visited her every day whenever she was hospitalized, except for the first seventy-two hours of her psychiatric hospitalizations and one night when my cab got into an accident on our way to the hospital. At home, I tucked her into bed each night and slept on the blue plastic-covered couch outside her bedroom or on the recliner chair and ottoman I pushed together to form a makeshift bed across from her bed. I was always exhausted, but I was holding it together. Facing Granny's death was a different kind of hard. I did not yet know that being smart or independent or "having it all together" isn't enough to hold you up under the weight of sadness your loved one will leave behind.

The doctor's questions reminded me of my family members and friends who always asked me, "Do you have a boyfriend?" or "When are you going to get married?"—as if my life would not begin, be worthwhile, or be complete until I was married. As if I, alone, were unimportant and unworthy of attention or celebration. I once emailed a former supervisor to update her on the happenings in my life. Like myself, she was an avid reader so I also included some info about a few books I'd recently read that she might enjoy.

"Instead of sending me a book report, you ought to be trying to find a husband," she responded. She was an older, married Black woman of the Jack-and-Jill bourgeoisie variety. Marrying well and keeping up appearances were everything to her. I was hurt that she didn't think anything I had to say was worth reading or listening to unless it was accompanied by an engagement or wedding announcement. Getting married was the least of my concerns. I was busy doing other things like getting established in my legal career, caring for Granny, and enjoying life. Since I didn't have any marriage updates, I stopped contacting my former supervisor.

Some women use the illusion of men's support to justify being in romantic relationships or staying in unhealthy relationships. A few years before Granny passed away, I'd contemplated breaking up with my then-boyfriend Darnell because he had done some not-so-nice thing or another. My friend Alexis, a Black woman who was married, had gone to law school with Darnell and had hooked us up. In response to my venting about him, Alexis told me a story about her other friend whose mother had recently died.

"She was single and had to travel back from Singapore by herself to make funeral arrangements for her mom," Alexis told me. "See, Darnell may have his issues but if something happened to Granny, I'm pretty sure he'd be there."

I was pretty sure he wouldn't "be there." He struggled with being available during non-urgent times, so impromptu hospital, morgue, and funeral home runs would've been out of the question. My friend was well-intentioned. She had also been close to her grandmother, who passed away. She knew how important it was to not go through grief alone. Like Granny's doctor, Alexis wanted to ensure someone was there for me when Granny passed away. Rather than committing to be part of my support system, she suggested I stay in a toxic relationship to ensure I had my very own emotional support human. That was a friendship failure on multiple levels. I also wondered what foolishness she had put up with in her romantic relationships for the sake of having a man "be there." She thought, like so many women, that a woman needed to be in a romantic relationship, even an unfulfilling one, to have emotional support. Being in a relationship doesn't guarantee that you won't have to go through hard times alone or that you won't feel lonely in those hard times. I've learned that folks who are unavailable in good times shouldn't be counted on to show up for you in bad times. Darnell and I broke up a couple of months later.

When Granny's doctor asked about my relationship status with a man to assess my support system, I was annoyed because the assumptions underlying her question were not consistent with my idea of feminism. My feminism was about more than men and women having equal rights and equal pay. It was about more than women having bodily autonomy. My feminism meant that men are not women's default plan. Feminist women are strong and independent and do not need men. Women may desire men, we may date or marry men, some of our best friends may even be men—but we should not *need* men.

My feminism was shaped by the Strong Black Woman ideal I saw so many Black women embody. I grew up surrounded by Granny and other unmarried women who had weathered life's storms alone. They were single and cared for their children and grandchildren. They had been resilient, resourceful, and independent because they had to be. They taught me that *man* is not synonymous with emotional support because men were absent or rarely around.

However, I often conflated feminism with *hyper*independence. It's difficult for me to ask for help because I've always figured things out on my own. I'd dealt with Granny's illnesses since I was a small child and been her official caregiver intermittently since high school.

Watching her die was just one more thing I'd handle alone. Women's friendship and mutual aid were the crucial elements of my feminist upbringing I'd forgotten. Granny had cared for sick friends and their family members; prayed for them in the hospital; called to check on them; and taken meals to elderly friends. She'd accompanied friends to police stations, hospitals, and funeral homes to provide moral support. She'd loaned friends money to travel to their loved ones' funerals. Although most of the women I knew growing up were unpartnered, they'd performed similar acts of care for their friends. Granny and her friends relied on their village of women.

Support comes dressed up in all sorts of bodies. Standing in my grandmother's hospital room with her doctors, I had yet to learn that just because I *can* face life's toughest moments alone doesn't mean I *should*. Refusing to seek or accept support from others shouldn't be my default way of living.

What Not to Give Someone Who Has Breast Cancer

- ✓ Opinions about why they got breast cancer or how they could've avoided it
- ✓ Medical advice
- ✓ Advice about that natural remedy you or a friend of a friend of a neighbor's momma's brother's cousin on their daddy's side tried (and a double "no" if that person is now dead, because the remedy clearly did not work)
- ✓ Books on how they can heal themselves from breast cancer through affirmations, marijuana, vitamins, meditation, and yoga
- ✓ Judgment

The occasion of Alexis's bad relationship advice wasn't the first time I'd considered who might accompany me in Granny's final moments and in making her final arrangements. I'd had these types of conversations with several of my coworkers. One of them, Verna, told me about the day the hospital called to inform her that her mother had passed away.

"I was in the office when I got the call," she told me. "I couldn't go up there by myself, so Yvette came with me." Yvette was our boss.

Now that Granny was near death, I understood Verna's need for company. Death is scary. You don't want to face it alone.

Granny's doctors flashed wide, eager grins when they saw my friend Taylor sitting beside me in Granny's room.

"Oh, we're so glad someone's here with you," said the doctor who had previously inquired about my marital status. Taylor worked at my job and drove me to the hospital so often that my usual cab driver Muhktar would get jealous. He glared at Taylor whenever he saw me walking to Taylor's car.

The doctors also rejoiced when my friend Ayesha, who I'd known since college, came and stayed with me for a few hours.

"I know it must be so hard to be losing your best friend," she had said a few days prior. "Have you talked to the doctors about end-of-life decisions, like a do-not-resuscitate order?" Ayesha was a social worker and knew what lay ahead.

"The social worker asked me if I wanted to sign one when Granny was first admitted, but I didn't sign it." I had still hoped Granny would pull through.

Ayesha came to visit Granny and me at the hospital a few days later. "Anything in particular you wanna eat?" she asked me, since she'd be arriving at dinnertime.

"As long as it's soul food, it doesn't matter." Nothing comforts you like macaroni and cheese and collard greens. When she arrived, we sat in Granny's room for a little while and then went to a lounge area to talk and eat. That's when I discovered that, after getting off work in New Jersey, Ayesha traveled by public transportation to a soul food restaurant in the city to pick up food for me, and then took more trains and buses to visit Granny and me in Brooklyn. She had traveled for at least three hours on a weeknight to see us.

In her essay "Ruth and Naomi, David and Jonathan," June Jordan writes about the support she received from her women friends during her breast cancer journey. She says, "This is the love of women. This is the mighty love that is saving my life." I learned to lean on the mighty, lifesaving love of my women friends when I needed them most.

Friends accompanied me to my first appointment with each breast surgeon I considered. After the first surgeon performed a breast exam and estimated how large my tumor was, she explained my surgical and post-surgery treatment options. I asked questions I'd written in my Leuchtturm1917 notebook while Joella took notes on her phone and interjected with her own questions. When we later discussed the visit and she texted me her notes, I was grateful that she had captured information I'd missed.

I saw another surgeon for a second opinion. Janine accompanied me to that visit. When you visit a breast surgeon, they use a diagram of a pair of breasts and lymph nodes to illustrate the location of the cancer cells. The diagram also includes other information like the clinical stage of your cancer, the types of hormone receptors on your cancer cells, surgical and treatment options, and types of referrals. Janine and I sat in front of the surgeon and looked at the page as she drew, highlighted, and wrote on the diagram. We tried to keep up as she explained the benefits of a lumpectomy and radiation versus a mastectomy. After meeting with the doctor, we returned to the waiting room so the receptionist could schedule my appointments for a breast MRI, genetic testing, and genetic counseling. We sat there as I completed the five-page family history questionnaire the hospital would need for my genetic counseling appointment.

I discussed surgeons and treatment options with Janine, Joella, Paige, and Safiya. I asked both surgeons additional questions about my MRI and getting a mastectomy. I also worried that if we had a surge in COVID-19 infections, hospitals might postpone all non-essential surgeries as they had done earlier in the pandemic. Breast cancer surgery was considered non-essential. I was afraid of making the wrong choice. It's hard worrying about cancer recurrence, hedging my bets, and balancing my fears against the confident optimism of my doctors. In the end, I chose the first surgeon and decided to have a lumpectomy.

When I woke up that Monday morning, I knew it was just a matter of hours. I had a foreboding feeling.

Unable to sleep after the previous night's visit, I had called the hospital at three o'clock that morning.

"How is my Granny doing?" I had asked the nurse.

"The same." That wasn't a good sign.

After being out of the office for a week to spend it with Granny in the ICU, I decided to go to work that morning to tie up a few loose ends and planned to leave work by noon to go back to the hospital. I wrote an out-of-office message for my email and turned it on. When my friend Paige called to check on me, I told her how hard it was to come to terms with the fact that Granny was dying. We cried together on the phone.

At around 10:30 AM, I called the hospital again to check on Granny.

"How is she doing?" I asked her nurse.

"She doesn't look good. She's having a hard time breathing." By this time, Granny wasn't breathing on her own at all and was completely reliant on the respirator.

"Is she in any pain?"

"No," the nurse replied. By this point, one month since she'd first been admitted to the hospital, keeping her comfortable and pain-free was the best anyone could hope for.

"Okay. I'll be up there soon to see her."

Although I'd planned to leave work by noon, I hurried through my tasks and left earlier. It was only a matter of time.

"How's grandma?" my coworker Lori asked as I passed her desk on the way to my office.

"Not good," I replied softly, my sadness stored in my raised eyebrows and tight lips. I kept walking. I couldn't stop to talk, or the tears would come.

My boss Gilbert came to my office.

"How are you doing?" he asked.

I wanted to reply, "I'm devastated. I can't imagine life without my Granny."

"Fine," I responded instead.

I got up from my desk and opened the file cabinet to the right of me, pretending I needed to get something out of it.

"Well, if you need to talk, I'm here," he said while getting up to leave.

"Thanks," I replied with a shaky voice and water pooling in my eyes. I smiled and gave him a thumbs-up as he left. He had that uncomfortable "maybe I should leave because she's about to have a freak out moment" look some men get when a woman is about to cry or get emotional. I knew he understood how I felt, because he had recently lost his mother, with whom he was very close. But I didn't want to talk.

Knowing what I might face at the hospital and not wanting to face it alone, I scrolled through my phone contacts for someone I could call to go with me to the hospital. But I couldn't find anyone. Not one person. At least, that's what I told myself. My hyperindependence had kicked in again. I could've asked one of my coworkers to go with me. We were a close-knit bunch and they asked about Granny every day. I could've also asked Taylor, who worked in another department at my job. But I thought about all the reasons not to ask him: I didn't want to burden him; I didn't think his supervisor would look too kindly on him leaving work so suddenly; it wasn't as if I was going to identify Granny's body. I wanted to save my lifeline for true emergencies and not waste them on the times leading up to the emergencies.

I called a cab and talked to my friend Samantha on the phone during the ride to the hospital.

"You sound like you're dragging yourself," she said.

"I am." I felt dread and heaviness. Dizzy. Lightheaded. I felt as if I were having an out-of-body experience, floating to the inevitable. The familiar shortness of breath. *I suppose some journeys must be traveled alone*, I thought.

I was too late. Granny passed away several minutes before I got to her room. I kissed her face and hands. I rubbed her stomach and the raised mole on the right side of Granny's neck, both soft and yielding to my touch. This was the last time I'd get to hold her. I was a child again. I sobbed as I bent down and wrapped my arms around her. I nestled my face in the crook of her neck. Granny's regular nurse came in and disconnected machines. Once I was standing again, a Black nurse came up beside me and rubbed my back as I continued to cry. She never said a word. This was the first time I'd ever seen her.

I cried as I called Granny's best friend Sister Christine and told her the news. Next, I called Aunt Chris.

"She's gone," was all I could say when she answered the phone. She cried with me.

"I'll tell Bill," she said. "Keep talking to her. The hearing is the last to go."

I told Granny how much I loved her and that I would miss her.

"I'm going to plan your going away party now," I told her before leaving her room for the last time.

I shook her doctor's hand and thanked him for caring for Granny.

"We tried everything we could," he said.

"I know." And they had. It just wasn't enough.

I looked for Granny's regular nurse before I left.

"A man was up here earlier," she said. "He stayed up here a long time. He sang to her and prayed in her room." I knew right away that it was Granny's friend Phil who had visited her. I'm glad Granny wasn't alone. I hope she heard him and knew she was loved right up to the end.

"Where's the other nurse?"

"Who?"

"She was a Black woman with short curly hair."

"I don't know who that is." I looked at the nearby nurse's station and didn't see her.

"Take care of yourself," Granny's nurse said as she hugged me goodbye.

Although I searched the entire unit, I never found the angel nurse who came in to console me.

With my eyes still blurred with tears, I walked out into the bright sunny afternoon and called a cab. I had a party to plan. A party fit for a queen.

I got a COVID test four days before my breast cancer surgery. Afterwards, I engaged in some retail therapy at Barnes & Noble and the farmers' market across the street. I bought a carved wood painting from the Senegalese artist Akassa in Union Square Park. The Black woman in the painting has a big, sculpted black Afro with flecks of aqua and brown in it. She sits naked with her chin resting on her left hand, with her left leg crossed over her right one. She and her small bare breasts remind me of myself. She represents normalcy and my "before"—the time before my breast was invaded by a tumor and runaway cancer cells, when it was unmarred by scalpels, stitches, and scar tissue. With books and bare-chested woman in hand, I ordered an Uber and headed home.

When most folks get into a cab or rideshare service, they put their headphones on, talk on the phone, read, sleep, or engage in some other activity that makes it clear they do not want to talk. I, on the other hand, am very talkative and have had the most interesting conversations with drivers. We've talked about what women look for when dating (based on my friends; I've given up because dating is one big shit show); how to grow orchids (I wish I'd taken better notes); gentrification (when you see yoga mats and Starbucks, it's a wrap); Brazilian butt lift surgeries (he recommended just losing weight the old fashioned way); and the filters Instagram models use (he dated a lot of IG models and said they don't look the same in person). Many of these conversations have ended with a "Why are you single?" (*Because I value peace of mind and y'all play too much*) or "Can I have your number?" (*No*). This Uber ride would be no different.

My driver was a Jamaican man named Harris.

"Your food smells so good I may have to jack you up for it," I told him. He was eating curried chicken, rice and peas, and plantains.

He laughed.

"You coming from work?" he asked.

"Nope. I just ran some errands and had a doctor's appointment."

"I hope everything's okay."

"Oh yeah, everything's fine. I just needed to get a COVID test to

get cleared for surgery." *Fine, if you consider breast cancer to be "fine."*
But who's counting?

"What kind of surgery are you having?" *He apparently talks as*
much as I do. It was a reasonable follow-up question.

"For breast cancer." *May as well tell all my business since I'm never*
going to see him again.

"Oh, I'm so sorry," he replied. "My daughter's mom is going
through that now." *This is where the conversation really took off.*

"Wow, I'm sorry. How's she doing?"

"She's going through chemo now. We're not together anymore,
but she's living with me. She was living alone and I didn't want my
daughter to worry," he explained.

He told me how they discovered she had breast cancer.

"She'd just had a mammogram a few months before and everything was fine," he said. "But then she had this lump under her arm
that wouldn't go away. I'm in nursing school so I knew something
was up. I told her she should get that checked out." It turns out she
had Stage 3 breast cancer, despite having a normal mammogram a
few months prior.

Harris gave me practical tips for coping with my recovery:
"Journal your thoughts; start meditating; save up enough money to
pay your bills for the few months that you won't be able to work; and
buy soursop tea to help with the side effects of the chemo and your
medications."

"These meds can cause vaginal dryness too." Although he was
correct, I remained quiet. Even *I* have my conversation limits. I draw
the line at dry coochies.

"Are you married?"

"No, but I have a boyfriend." *I guess this was the next logical ques-*
tion after talking about vaginal dryness.

"Okay, good," he replied. "This is where your man will have to
prove himself. Even though you have a man, have your family ready

to help out if necessary. If he leaves while you're going through all of this, fuck him. If he stays with you through all of this, then you know he's the one. After everything is over, you tell him, 'Nigga, I'ma marry you!'"

I laughed so hard.

I had also lied. I didn't have a boyfriend, or even a booty call/ come-put-these-bookshelves-together dude on standby. I lied because I didn't want a pity party from him. I also didn't want him to ask a bunch of questions about how I would manage my surgery, treatments, and recovery without having a partner at home. Nor did I want to have one of those "Why is someone like you single?" conversations men are so good at starting. Although he had asked about my relationship status, he also acknowledged that relationships and support from partners don't always last through the hard times. I appreciated that he gave me tips on how to cope with breast cancer that I could use as a single woman. He didn't end the conversation after he thought I had a man at home, as if that were all I might need.

Harris parked in front of my apartment building, and we talked for several more minutes as my next-door neighbor nosily peered into the car from the steps he was sitting on nearby.

"If you can't find the soursop tea, let me know and I'll buy it and bring it to you." This was such a generous gesture, considering that he was a stranger and lived in the Bronx, over an hour away from my Brooklyn apartment. This conversation was just what I needed. It helped ease some of my anxieties. Harris understood, better than most, what I would face in the coming months. His words were honest, kind, and practical.

"You have such great energy and a great attitude. It'll help you as you recover," he said. We texted each other a month later. I updated him on how my surgery had gone. His daughter's mother was doing well. That's an Uber conversation for which I will always be grateful.

I walked to the funeral home to make Granny's final arrangements. Sister Christine stayed on speakerphone with me as I picked out Granny's white casket with pink accents and told the funeral director which amenities I wanted to include: pink-and-white prayer cards with, on one side, praying hands to match the praying hands on the plaque inside her casket and, on the other side, Psalm 121, one of her favorite scriptures ("I will lift up mine eyes unto the hills, from whence cometh my help. My help cometh from the Lord . . ."); and pink-and-white programs in the form of 8 1/2"-by-11" booklets that would include pictures of Granny and a list of her favorite sayings. Later that day, my neighbor Gail stopped by to sit with me and eat Chinese food. That night, as I sat flipping through Granny's phone book looking for the telephone numbers of people I would have to call with funeral details, my doorbell rang. It was Paige, who had driven from New Jersey with flowers to see me. She had never been to my house in the almost ten years we had known each other.

Safiya and Samantha both arrived two days after Granny left me. Although we talked often, I had not seen Safiya since our law school graduation six years earlier. Whenever Safiya called the house phone, she'd talk to Granny. Sometimes Granny even threw in a good prayer. I had only seen Samantha in person once or twice, having met her online a few years earlier on a social networking site. Granny began showing signs of Alzheimer's disease around the time Samantha and I met online. When I told her about my difficulty getting Granny properly assessed, she contacted the Alzheimer's Association to see what assistance they could provide me. Through Samantha's efforts, we were referred to the Brooklyn Memory Clinic.

Afraid Granny's ghost and invisible friends might wander, both Safiya and Samantha refused to sleep in my bedroom on the second floor. So, we all slept downstairs—Safiya on the home attendants' bed in the living room, Samantha on the couch across from Safiya, and me in Granny's room a few feet away. Although they had never met, they stayed up late talking long after I fell asleep.

Safiya and Samantha helped me run errands as we prepared for Granny's funeral. We picked out Granny's last outfit, a pink suit we saw in Soon Soon, Granny's favorite dress shop. It was fancy, just like Granny—a satin embroidered pattern of little diamonds covered the jacket and skirt; small satin flowers with a single pink cubic zirconia at their center covered the cuffs and cloth that went across her chest. They didn't judge me or fuss when I announced that we'd have to travel across town to buy a tiara for Granny to wear because she loved looking and being treated like a queen. Queen Anne was one of my nicknames for her. Every year, I threw Granny a birthday party to which she always wore a tiara. I had started the tradition three birthdays earlier for her 72nd birthday, after she had a joint party in Florida with her twin brother. She felt left out at the party because most of the attendees were her brother's friends. When we got back to New York, I threw a party for her in her friend Mother King's backyard and bought her a tiara so she would feel extra special. For weeks after, she still wore her birthday tiara around the house. She had just worn one at her birthday party two months before her death. She would still be a queen at her going away party.

When we hailed a cab, I recognized the Puerto Rican driver. He used to take me to work every morning.

"My grandmother just passed away," I told him.

"I sah-ree, mami. Rest in peace, abuelita," he replied. We laughed as he recounted the day he had picked Granny and her home attendant up to drive them to the courthouse downtown to see me get sworn in as an attorney several years earlier. That morning, I had gone ahead of them because the new attorneys were required to be there early. The plan was simple: Granny and her home attendant were supposed to take a cab and arrive in time for the swearing-in ceremony. Instead, her home attendant called to tell me Granny refused to get into the cab because she was afraid they were taking her to the psychiatric unit at the hospital to be admitted instead of to the courthouse. I listened as the cab driver and several of our neighbors pleaded with Granny to get into the cab and told her no one was going to lock her up or hurt her. She eventually got in, and they arrived shortly after the ceremony started. Granny stood up with her coat on and held her cane tightly in front of her for the entire ceremony. Seeing the cab driver again that day was comforting. He was our Batmobile, heaven-sent at the right time. It was as if Granny had orchestrated the entire thing.

We finally arrived at the store and picked out a tiara. I purchased two, just in case one broke. We designated Safiya as the tiara-bearer. Her only job was to make sure they made it to the funeral home that evening in one piece. At Black homegoings, the deceased usually has her hands resting on a Bible. Granny would be no exception. The three of us gasped when we spotted the last pink suede Bible on a shelf. "That's the one," Safiya said. It perfectly matched Granny's suit and casket. We picked out white lace gloves for Granny. She would also need traveling shoes. I picked out a pair of silver sparkly ones because Granny loved fancy things that glittered.

Gift Ideas for Someone Who Has Breast Cancer

- ✓ Soft blankets
- ✓ Furry slippers or soft non-slip socks
- ✓ Gift cards for a ridesharing app, food-delivery app, dog-walking service, or housecleaning service
- ✓ Their favorite foods
- ✓ Face masks

- ✓ Incense and candles
- ✓ Books
- ✓ Flowers or plants
- ✓ The names of support groups or other people they can talk to who've had breast cancer
- ✓ Phone calls to check in

I had Granny's homegoing at a small funeral home close to our house. I was overwhelmed with gratitude by the number of people who came—my family on my maternal grandfather's side; friends I had gone to school with; coworkers; Granny's friends, most of whom had known me all my life, many of whom had even known my mother as a child; Granny's caseworker; her two favorite home attendants, Robin and Paola.

Although they hated public speaking, Samantha and Safiya filled in where there was no one designated on the funeral program to perform a particular task, including reading Bible scriptures and Granny's obituary. I cried as the officiant, a family friend, sang a song whose title I have long forgotten. Her father, Granny's longtime friend who preached her eulogy and had known her since before I was born, sat beside me and held my hand as I cried. Granny's homegoing was a celebration. The order of service wasn't always orderly and we didn't care. The attendees all talked longer than their allotted two minutes. They didn't wait for the funeral director to announce that it was time to view Granny's body. They simply got up and formed a line. The hospital chaplain who had visited and prayed for Granny spoke of Granny's Pentecostal faith, which is full of shouting and dancing and speaking in tongues. She talked about how Granny would have loved to see me dance in the spirit. She then came over to me, grabbed my hands and pulled me up. The organist played some fast, shouting music and we danced a holy dance. One last dance for Granny.

"I'm so glad I no longer have to give myself these injections," I told the oncology nurse as she took my vitals and prepared the medication. The health insurance at my new job covered my monthly hospital-administered Lupron injections. However, my previous job's health insurance did not, so I had to stick myself in the butt each month.

"You should write about what it's like to go through cancer treatment as a single woman."

Giving myself Lupron injections was another one of those life events that reminded me of my singleness. I sometimes stared at my dog, Buster, and wondered if I could teach him to administer my shots. It would've been too weird to ask a neighbor for assistance.

Each month, I had to mentally prepare myself before each injection. The entire ordeal was a hot-ass mess, literally and figuratively. It was a lot of work to locate the injection site on my butt, make sure the long, thin needle stayed at a 90-degree angle and didn't bend on the way in, and ensure I'd inserted it into the muscle. Each time I injected myself, I worked up a sweat and did so much twisting and turning that it felt like I had sprained muscles in my neck, arms, stomach, back, and fat rolls. I swear there are a million little muscles deep inside those rolls around my waist.

My friend Safiya was my injection companion. She added my injection dates to her own calendar and sent me "Girl, it's almost booty-shot day" texts. My first self-administered injection was quite an ordeal. Safiya googled injection instructions from her home in California, while I stood bottomless and looked at the instructions the pharmacy had given me. In addition to the trauma of having to give myself injections, I was also at the mercy of the dizzying inefficiencies of middle-age. I was forty-two, nearsighted, and in denial about my need for bifocals, so I had to take my glasses off to read the small print on the instructions and then put my glasses back on so I could see well enough to prepare the syringe and inject myself. It took more time to read and understand the instructions and prepare the medication than it did to give myself the shot.

"I don't think the bottom part is supposed to have liquid in it."

"Which stopper am I supposed to push to the blue line?"

After I got through mixing the powder and diluent and checking for clumps of powder, it took forever for me to figure out how to remove the needle cap.

We were finally ready for the injection.

"I'm bleeding. How do I know if it went into the muscle?" I asked Safiya.

"Well, if you're bleeding and the medicine didn't spill anywhere, it must've went in."

"Yeah, I guess you're right." Neither one of us were doctors, but she sounded correct. I had a bloody, sore ass. I was emotionally spent.

Even if no one was there to help me in person, at least Safiya could laugh and read instructions along with me, and lament about my booty-shot woes. Now I happily go to the breast center every month to have my booty shots administered by the professionals. In the spring and summer, I leave the clinic and go eat a celebratory vanilla ice cream cone with chocolate sprinkles under a tree. It's the little things.

Instead of the customary repast folks have after funerals, a few friends and I decided to have dinner at the same soul food restaurant in the city Ayesha had bought my food from the day she visited the hospital. But first we removed the flowers that covered and surrounded Granny's casket and brought them back to my house. It was Samantha's idea. She was a gardener and said flowers would brighten up the place and bring good energy. The flowers would have otherwise been thrown out because Granny's body was being taken to Florida, where we would have a second funeral for her that our family could attend, and then she would be buried there. It was then that I noticed all the vases around the house, yet we rarely, if ever, bought flowers. Growing up, Granny always said she was allergic to them. Her birthday party a couple of months prior was the first time I remembered buying her flowers. I'd informed everyone that we'd be having a floral theme and asked them to bring her some. She didn't sneeze or show any other symptoms of allergies that day.

After her funeral, my friends and I placed the flowers in vases throughout the house—the dining room, kitchen, living room, bathroom, Granny's room. And then someone made restaurant reservations and those with cars mapped out driving directions on their respective phones. We were finally on our way to dinner in the city.

The restaurant was a small storefront with a broken air conditioner. The place was so small that the nine of us filled it, leaving no room for additional customers to sit. It was so hot I took off my suit jacket, wearing only the camisole beneath, my straightened hair sticking to my face. We sat sweating in the July night heat. We ate macaroni and cheese and collard greens and fried chicken and meatloaf and chocolate cake. We laughed, talked, and reminisced. We talked about how we had all met. We laughed at the memory of Granny dancing and singing along with Frank Sinatra to "New York, New York" during my law school's 50th anniversary gala. We laughed at her knack for butchering my friends' names, and her habit of picking up the phone in the middle of my conversations to tell me, "Dinner is ready. Clean your room!" We reminisced about Granny's invisible friends and funny moments from her going away party. The day of Granny's homegoing wasn't what I had imagined or planned, but it was perfect. In that cramped restaurant in Chelsea, Granny's spirit hovered around me and seeped between the notes of our laughter, stories, plate scraping, and the background music. In the end, I was unwed, uncoupled, single. And yet, I was loved.

Acknowledgments

To my grandmother, Annie Lee McKinney, I would not be who I am, be the writer I am, without you. You were the first storyteller I knew and my first reader. Granny Poo, thank you for teaching me that my stories are worthy of being told. Thank you for nurturing my love of reading and writing, for always giving me money to buy books at the school bookfairs, and for showing me that writing is another way to mourn and talk to God.

To my mother, Cheryl Ann Savage, you asked me to help you tell your story. I hope I have done you proud. Thank you for giving me life and for being you, unapologetically, to the end.

To my godmother, Christine Jones, thank you for being Granny's best friend until her last breath, for being a mother to me after she passed away, and for always encouraging me to write. You said you'd be onstage with me when my first book was published. I wish you, Granny, and Cheryl could've been here physically, but I know you are always with me in spirit.

To my father, Justin Savage, thank you for falling in love with Cheryl all those years ago and for being the father I need today. I love you.

Uncle Bill, thank you for being the keeper of our family's stories and legacy. Thank you for reading all my essays, sharing them with family members, and sharing your thoughts about my writing.

Aunt Chris, thank you for always being a soft place for our family to land and for giving me great childhood memories.

Aunt Dot, thank you for your love and support and for being with me on one of the hardest days of my life.

To my brilliant literary agent, Mariah Stovall, thank you for be-lieving in me and my writing, for your compassion, for being a fierce advocate, and for giving me the kind of edits and feedback that make me rethink my entire existence. When we first spoke, you told me that my only job was to write well and that everything else would work itself out. You were right. Thank you.

Many thanks to the rest of the wonderful team at Trellis Literary Management.

To Matthew Specktor, thank you for your time and your wise and encouraging words.

To the incredible team at HarperCollins, past and present, who helped bring this book into the world, thank you! Two snaps in the air for my current editor, Adenike Olanrewaju, and former editor, Sarah Ried, who acquired this book. Editors are out here doing the work of the Lord, and I am so grateful for both of you. Adenike, thank you for patiently and graciously shepherding me through this publishing process. Shout out to editorial assistant extraordinaire Liz Velez. Thank you for all that you do and for always making sure things flow smoothly. It takes more than an author's words to make a beautiful book. Many thanks to Joanne O'Neill, Jen Overstreet, Stacey Fischkelta, and Michael Fierro for all their hard work. To Karintha Parker and Megan Looney, thank you for working hard to ensure that as many people as possible will get to meet the women in this book.

Thank you to the educators who have helped me find and shape my words. To my sixth-grade teacher, Mrs. Steinberg, thank you for igniting my love for poetry and desire to be a writer. To my high school English teacher, Dr. Weinberger, thank you for seeing my potential and sending me to poetry workshops in the city. To Dr. Judith Weisenfeld, my religion professor at Barnard College, thank you for inspiring me to write about my experiences in the Pentecostal church. My Barnard crew and I still talk about your classes all these years later. To Kiese Laymon, my instructor at Rivendell Writers' Colony, thank you for showing me how to be honest in my work and how to celebrate and lovingly critique the people and communities

I love. To Charles D'Ambrosio, my workshop instructor at the Tin House Winter Workshop, thank you for helping me quell my self-doubt when you told me, "You have to stop thinking you're not ready to write this book, because you are."

To Michele Filgate, in whose class I wrote the first essay in this book, thank you for introducing me to a community of other writers and for being so wonderful and supportive in every phase of my writing career. Thank you for also modeling what an inclusive writing workshop is like.

To Megan Stielstra, who wrote the following when she signed her book for me nearly six years ago: "Listen: next time I'll hold your book in my hands and you'll sign it for me"—I've looked at your encouraging note over the years whenever I had doubts about my writing or thought about giving up. Thank you for those words. I can't wait to sign my book for you.

To Marita Golden, thank you for your words, your work, and your teaching. Thank you for encouraging me to ask the questions that revealed the book I really wanted to write.

To Shanon Lee: Girl, if it weren't for you, I'd still be reading books about how to write a book proposal instead of actually writing my book proposal. Thank you for setting up our book proposal group, for all your support on this journey, and your friendship.

To Briallen Hopper, Danielle A. Jackson, Alison Kinney, and Jessica Wilbanks, thank you for always championing me and my work.

To Edwidge Danticat, Rachel Eliza Griffiths, Joan Didion, June Jordan, and Audre Lorde, thank you for showing me how to write about the loved ones and things I've lost and for writing words that bring me solace and courage.

To Zora Neale Hurston, bell hooks, Toni Morrison, Ntozake Shange, Claudia Rankine, and Alice Walker, thank you for showing me more possibilities and a way forward with your words.

I've been blessed to receive support from many wonderful organizations. Thank you to Gotham Writers Workshop, Catapult, Tin House, Rivendell Writers' Colony, the Writers' Colony at Dairy Hollow, and Storyknife Writers Retreat.

To the New York University Creative Writing Program, I'm proud to be among you. Thank you for your support.

Thank you to the journals and magazines who've published my work.

To all the writers who've read and workshopped my essays, thank you for your generosity and insights.

I wrote part of this book while undergoing treatment for breast cancer. To my doctors, nurses and nurse practitioners, and all the techs, receptionists, and everyone else who impacted my care and experience at Mount Sinai Hospital, thank you! Thank you for taking me apart and putting me back together so that I could be here to write this book and many more to come.

To photographer Sylvie Rosokoff, makeup artist Melissa Drouillard, my barber Sherman and hairstylist Tee, thank you for making me look and feel amazing.

To the dynamic duo Jennifer Bailey and Joella Ocasio, words are not enough to express my gratitude and love for you two. Thank you for always being there when I need you most.

To Jennifer Abcug, thank you for lending me your ears and support over the years. Thank you for encouraging me to dream new dreams.

To my East New York family, including Gail Goode, Gwen Wilkinson, Eddie Goode, Mother Daisy King, Norma Smith, and Nancy Graulau, thank you for loving Granny and me. It takes a village to love a senior. Thank you for being part of ours.

To Shaquiea Sykes, I would sing the *Golden Girls* theme song right now, but we both know that singing is not my ministry. Thank you for being my friend, for reading my essay drafts, and being down for all my shenanigans (that do not involve singing).

To Aleia McDaniel, thank you for all the pep talks and words of affirmation you've given me since our first year at Barnard. Thank you for telling me that it's okay to abandon the book I thought I wanted to write for the book I really want to write.

To Karima Burns and Tené Smith, thank you for being there for me through the ups and the downs, for letting me cry and crying with me, and for being my sisters from different misters.

To Danielle Barrett, Janel George, Latasha George, Janelle Hobson, Tiffany Lyttle, Sue Rock, Curtis Stallworth, and Junea Williams, thank you for giving me, as June Jordan says, "the mighty love that is saving my life."

To Heather McClean and Barbara Van Norden, thank you for talking me through the hardest part of writing this book.

To Mayra E. Bell and Jessica K. Cooke, thank you for your friendship and support.

To everyone who has listened to me go on and on about this book, attended readings of mine, given me encouraging words, or supported me in other ways—thank you!

I am immensely grateful to the writers who've taken time away from their own work and lives to read this book and write blurbs for me.

To everyone who reads this book, thank you for spending time with my words and my jaybirds. I hope you enjoy the journey.

About the Author

Jodi M. Savage is a writer and attorney whose essays have appeared in the *Huffington Post, Catapult, Kweli Journal,* the *VIDA Review, WSQ Journal,* and elsewhere. She is a Goldwater Fellow and an MFA candidate in creative nonfiction at New York University. She lives in Brooklyn, New York.